THE Q & A GUIDE TO
MENTAL PRAYER

Connie Rossini

Four Waters Press
OMAHA, NEBRASKA

Scripture verses are taken from the Catholic Edition of the Revised Standard Version of the Bible, © 1965, 1966 by the Division of Christian Education of the National Council of the Churches of Christ in the United States of America. Used by permission. All rights reserved.

Quotes from St. Teresa of Ávila's *Interior Castle, The Way of Perfection,* and *The Life of St. Teresa by Herself,* unless otherwise noted, are from the E. Allison Peers Editions, which are in the Public Domain.

Quotes from St. John of the Cross are from *The Collected Works of St. John of the Cross,* Translated by Kieran Kavanaugh, OCD and Otilio Rodriguez, OCD. Washington, DC: ICS Publications, © 1991.

Catechism quotes are taken from *Catechism of the Catholic Church* (2nd ed.). Washington, DC: Libreria Editrice Vaticana-United States Conference of Catholic Bishops, © 2000.

Four Waters Press
11015 Fowler Avenue
Omaha, NE 68164

Special discounts are available on large quantity purchases by associations, book clubs, and others. Contact the Publisher at the address above.

ISBN: 978-0-9972023-4-2

To the members of my Facebook group,
Authentic Contemplative Prayer,
May God fulfill your greatest desires!

Contents

Introduction... 1

The Basics of Christian Prayer

1. What is prayer?... 5

2. What is Christian prayer?....................................... 6

3. Why should I pray?... 7

4. What are the forms of Christian prayer?.............. 9

5. What are the three expressions of personal
   prayer?... 9

6. What is vocal prayer?... 10

7. What is meditation? 11

8. What is contemplation?.. 11

Mental Prayer and Meditation

9. What is mental prayer?... 13

10. Is mental prayer more effective than vocal
    prayer? 15

11. Can I pray mental prayer aloud? 16

12. Is mental prayer the same thing as meditation?....... 16

13. Is praying spontaneously throughout the day a
    form of mental prayer?..................................... 17

14. Is meditation the same as Bible study? 17

15. Can I practice both meditative and Charismatic prayer? 18

16. Are vocal prayer and mental prayer mutually exclusive? 19

17. Why is meditation important? 21

18. If I can only do mental prayer or go to daily Mass, which should I choose? 22

19. If I pray the Rosary daily, why do I still have to pray mental prayer? 25

20. What if I miss my mental prayer time? 27

Conditions for Prayer

21. How do I begin a life of prayer? 29

22. How can I establish a prayer habit? 29

23. How can I find time to pray? 31

24. What's the best time for prayer? 32

25. What's the best place for prayer? 33

26. What's the best posture for praying? 33

27. How long should I pray each day? 34

28. What are the immediate preparations for mental prayer? 35

29. What lifestyle best supports mental prayer? 37

30. How is virtue related to prayer? 37

31. What is detachment? 39

32. Why is detachment necessary? 41

33. How can I practice detachment? 42

Practicing Meditation

34. Is Lectio divina the same thing as meditation? 45

35. What should I do in the contemplatio step of Lectio divina? 46

36. What are some other methods of meditation? 47

37. What Scriptures should I choose for meditation?........................ 48

38. Should I use pre-made meditations or make my own? 49

39. What do I do when the Scripture moves me? 50

40. Are the imaginative types of prayer that the Jesuits teach useful? 50

41. Are there other ways to meditate besides using Scripture? 51

42. Are resolutions a necessary part of mental prayer? 52

Listening to God in Prayer

43. How is silence important for prayer? 55

44. How can I remain quiet to hear the voice of God?....................... 57

45. How might God speak to me during prayer? 58

46. How do I know that the voice I am hearing in prayer is really God?........................ 59

47. How can I allow the Holy Spirit to pray through me and for me?........................ 60

48. What if I am asking for guidance and God is silent? 61

The Experience of Mental Prayer

49. What are consolations in prayer? 63

50. What is desolation? 64

51. Should prayer normally be consoling and peaceful? 65

52. How do I know if my consolations come from God? 66

53. Should I empty myself in prayer? 67

54. Is it okay to listen to music while I pray? 68

55. Is it okay to spend my mental prayer time talking to God about my difficulties? 70

56. Can mental prayer be a communal activity? 71

57. Can mental prayer be addressed to a saint or the Blessed Virgin Mary? 72

58. Should prayer before the Blessed Sacrament be different than prayer at home? 72

59. What if I experience visions or locutions during prayer? 73

60. Is there a connection between dreams and mental prayer? 75

61. What if God does not answer my prayers? 76

Difficulties in Meditation

62. Why is it sometimes so hard to meditate? 79

63. What should I do when I cannot recollect myself for prayer? 80

64. If I seem to get nothing out of my meditation, how should I spend my time? 81

65. What if I'm too drowsy when I pray? 81

66. Is it okay to drink coffee when I pray? 82

67. How can I pray with brain fog caused by illness? 83

68. How can I overcome distractions? 83

69. How can I overcome lustful and blasphemous
     thoughts in prayer? 85

70. Why does it seem nothing happens in my
     prayer until the last five minutes? 87

Meditation: Christian Versus Non-Christian

71. How is Christian meditation different from
     eastern (non-Christian) meditation? 89

72. Is eastern meditation a help or a hindrance? 90

73. Is mindfulness compatible with mental prayer? 92

74. Is it okay to use mantras in prayer? 95

75. Isn't the Jesus Prayer a mantra? 97

76. What is Centering Prayer? 98

77. How is Centering Prayer problematic? 99

78. Did Teresa of Ávila suggest something like
     Centering Prayer? 102

79. What has the Church said about eastern
     meditation? 104

80. Has the Church addressed Centering Prayer or
     the use of mantras? 107

81. Is Yoga an acceptable practice? 108

The Different Stages of Christian Prayer

82. What are the nine grades of prayer? 111

83. What are the three stages of the spiritual life?........112

84. What are the different levels of meditative
      prayer?...113

85. What are the four waters of prayer? 117

86. How do Saint Teresa's mansions correlate with
      the grades of prayer?.......................................118

87. Should I know what spiritual stage I am in?.............120

88. Will I ever really leave the purgative way? 122

89. What signs mark the end of the purgative way? 123

Advancing in Prayer

90. How can I tell if I am making progress?....................125

91. Sometimes I feel moved to just silently adore
      God. Is this okay?...126

92. Is the prayer of recollection the same as
      practicing the presence of God?................127

93. What is the dark night of the soul?............................127

94. How is the passive night different from
      ordinary dryness? 129

95. How is the dark night different from other
      kinds of suffering? 130

96. What is a "dark desire" in prayer? 132

97. How can I work on the active night of the
      senses?...132

98. How should mortification change as I advance
      in prayer?...133

99. How can I keep from becoming attached to
      something new? 136

100. What should I do if I fall back?.................................137

Contemplative Prayer

101. Is meditation the same thing as
     contemplation? 139

102. What are alternate understandings of the
     word contemplation? 139

103. Is speaking in tongues contemplative prayer? 142

104. Is contemplation the same thing as hearing
     God speak to me? 143

105. How can I attain contemplation?.........................144

106. Can a person experience contemplation
     outside of mental prayer?.............................144

107. Can contemplation happen during Mass? 145

108. What is acquired contemplation?.........................146

109. How is acquired recollection different from
     infused recollection? 147

110. What does one experience when transitioning
     from meditation to contemplation?.........................148

111. Does God call everyone to contemplation? 149

112. Is contemplation rare?..150

113. Were all canonized saints contemplatives? 151

114. Why does God give some the gift of
     contemplation, but not others? 153

115. Should people refer to themselves as
     contemplatives?..156

116. What are the different levels of
     contemplation? 157

Miscellaneous Questions

117. Do I really need a spiritual director?........................159

118. How can I find a spiritual director?............................160

119. Why don't priests teach about mental prayer?.......160

120. Do non-Catholics have different ideas of
     prayer and prayer methods? 161

121. I seem to be growing lukewarm about prayer.
     How can I reignite the fire? 162

122. Is Bible study helpful for deepening my prayer
     life?...163

123. Can my temperament make mental prayer
     more difficult? 163

124. What does it mean to live a contemplative life? 165

125. How can I find support for living a
     contemplative life? 166

Acknowledgments 167

About the Author 169

Introduction

A mong the Catholic laity today there is a hunger for teaching on deep prayer. This hunger is not being filled by what they hear from the pulpit. Few priests know much about contemplation themselves. Most who do feel ill-equipped to teach it to others. Some bring in experts for parish missions. Many others allow problematic groups to hold retreats and ongoing meetings. Where, then, can the laity go for clear and orthodox teaching on prayer? Most turn to the writings of the saints, but these are often difficult to understand without help, especially for beginners in prayer. More recent books on Catholic spirituality tend to be either written for those who are just starting to give their lives to God, with no hint of the heights to which God calls us, or they teach a feel-good, New Age substitute. A few others are tomes that intimidate today's readers. Where are the contemporary, orthodox books about union with God for non-scholars? *The Q & A Guide to Mental Prayer* seeks to fill this gap.

When I began blogging about the spiritual life in 2012, I didn't know where that would take me. Having been a Secular Discalced Carmelite (OCDS) for seventeen years and a home educator for six, I called the blog Contemplative Homeschool. I went on to write several books about Catholic spirituality, including the premier critique of problematic prayer techniques (outside the magisterium itself), *Is Centering Prayer Catholic?* Then in 2016, at the request of a friend, I started a Facebook group focused on distinguishing between problematic practices like Centering Prayer and the true Catholic tradition. I called it Authentic Contemplative Prayer. Eventually the group morphed from focusing on negatives to positives, sharing the teachings of Saints Teresa of Ávila and John of the Cross on deepening prayer. Today over 11,000 members, about half of them active in any given week, discuss how they can grow in intimacy with Christ.

Over the past six-and-a-half years, I have been asked the same questions repeatedly. My answers have become more refined, more based on the experience of myself and countless others who have shared their joys and difficulties with me, rather than just coming from what I have read in books or been taught in a formation class. I decided to share these answers in a permanent format.

My hope is that many beginners in prayer will learn where to start by reading these pages. That those advancing in prayer will understand what God is doing in their souls and avoid common pitfalls. That priests and spiritual directors will find added confidence that what they are teaching is in accord with the saints. And that many will refer back to this book when searching for the answer to a specific question.

The experts on prayer

How can you be sure this book is a reliable guide to prayer? I am not a theologian, just a laywoman seeking to help others find the joy and peace I have found through prayer. My gift lies in taking difficult concepts and recrafting them in words the average person can understand. Few of the answers that follow are exclusively my own. They are based on the teachings of the Church, the saints, and respected spiritual theologians. Let me introduce you to the experts and explain why they are authoritative:

Saint Teresa of Ávila: Designated by the Church the "Doctor of Prayer," Teresa, more than any other person in history, gives expert teaching on the stages of prayer, what to expect in each of them, and how to keep growing.

Saint John of the Cross: Named the "Mystical Doctor," he is the authority on the stages of purification we must go through to reach union with God, and, with Saint Teresa, an expert in contemplation.

Saint Francis de Sales: The "Doctor of Charity," Francis wrote for lay men and women, applying teaching on prayer, virtue, and mortification in a practical and prudent manner.

Saint Alphonsus Liguori: "Most Zealous Doctor," his teaching on prayer can sometimes be out of reach for the average lay person, but on other matters he fills in gaps left by the other doctors.

Saint Ignatius of Loyola: Although he is not a doctor of the Church, his teaching on the Discernment of Spirits is unmatched.

The Desert Fathers: Christians of the third through fifth centuries, they sought solitude with God and a life of prayer in the desert. Their teaching on prayer is often less refined or systematic than those who came after them. It continues most noticeably in the eastern half of the Church.

The Congregation for the Doctrine of the Faith (CDF): As the Vatican congregation responsible for preserving the integrity of the Faith, the CDF issued the 1989 document *On Some Aspects of Christian Meditation.* It gives vital aid in avoiding errors on prayer.

Besides these are other obvious authorities such as documents from Ecumenical Councils and the *Catechism of the Catholic Church.*

In the nineteenth and twentieth centuries, the Dominican order produced some of the greatest spiritual theologians of modern times. From among these, I rely most heavily on Fr. Jordan Aumann and Fr. Reginald Garrigou-Lagrange. Two of the most insightful (and holy) Carmelite authors of the twentieth century are Fr. Gabriel of St. Mary Magdalen and Blessed (Père) Marie-Eugène. Among living authors, I have found Fr. Jacques Philippe and Daniel (Dan) Burke two of the most helpful for their simple, understandable teaching and orthodoxy.

These are my sources. Wherever possible, I have cited their works to support my answers.

May the Holy Spirit be with you as you read this book, inspiring you to give yourself to God without reservation!

The Basics of
Christian Prayer

1. What is prayer?

The *Catechism of the Catholic Church* (CCC) gives several definitions of prayer. One example is, "Prayer is the raising of one's mind and heart to God or the requesting of good things from God."[1] Everyone is familiar with requesting things from God. Making requests is often wordy prayer. "The raising of one's mind and heart to God" is a more difficult concept. It may not include any words at all. Yet, this raising (that is, offering) of the heart and mind is essential to every Christian prayer. Saint Teresa of Ávila said,

> If a person does not think Whom he is addressing, and what he is asking for, and who it is that is asking and of Whom he is asking it, I do not consider that he is praying at all even though he be constantly moving his lips. True, it is sometimes possible to pray without paying heed to these things, but that is only because they have been thought about previously; if a man is in the habit of speaking to God's

---

[1] CCC no. 2559, quoting St. John Damascene.

Majesty as he would speak to his slave, and never wonders if he is expressing himself properly, but merely utters the words that come to his lips because he has learned them by heart through constant repetition, I do not call that prayer at all — and God grant no Christian may ever speak to Him so![2]

An essential element of prayer is recognizing that God is greater than yourself. This is why saints speak of "raising" the heart and mind. You express to God what is in your mind or heart, implicitly recognizing that he has the power to aid you.

2. What is Christian prayer?

What makes Christian prayer different from the prayers offered by non-Christians? The Catechism says, "Prayer is *Christian* insofar as it is communion with Christ and extends throughout the Church, which is his Body."[3] Christian prayer comes from the mind and heart of one who has faith in Christ, one who is part of his Body, the Church. The deeper the prayer, the more this communion with Christ and his Church comes to fruition. Christ, the Mediator between God and man,[4] must be at the center of all Christian prayer. Without him, there can be no communion with God. He shares with you in prayer his own communion with the Father, through the Holy Spirit. He enables you to live in a union of love with God. In order to be called

---

[2] *Interior Castle* 1, 1.
[3] CCC no. 2565. Emphasis in the original.
[4] 1 Tim 2:5.

Christian, even the simplest of prayers must at least implicitly be offered through him.

3. Why should I pray?

Here are seven reasons you should pray daily:

1. Jesus, Mary, and all the saints prayed. Jesus prayed in at least fifteen passages in the Gospels. Luke 6:12 is typical: "In these days he went out into the hills to pray; and all night he continued in prayer to God." Jesus was God the Son, always united with the Father, yet, as a man, he found it necessary to pray. Mary is a model of prayer. Her Magnificat[5] is a profound prayer. We are told she "treasured all these things and reflected on them in her heart."[6] She truly prayed without ceasing. Pick up any saint's biography and you read about a life steeped in prayer. No matter the culture, the state in life, or the age of the saint, they all communed with God daily.

2. Prayer gives you self-knowledge. Without daily prayer, you will be blind to many of your sins and weaknesses. Prayer enables you to see yourself as you are, so you can work (with God's grace) to change.

3. Prayer keeps you from sin. Prayer gives you the grace to overcome present and future temptations. Saint John Chrysostom wrote, "It is impossible, utterly impossible, for

---

[5] Lk 1:46-55.
[6] Lk 2:19, et cetera.

the man who prays eagerly and invokes God ceaselessly ever to sin."[7]

4. Relationships need communication. Just as a friendship can fall apart without communication, if you seldom converse with God, you will easily fall away.

5. God always listens. No matter how much other people may turn a deaf ear to your concerns, God always hears you. Sincere prayer is always efficacious, even if God doesn't answer the way you want or expect.

6. Prayer disposes you to receive the sacraments. A person who prays is more likely to frequent the sacrament of Reconciliation and make a good Confession. Prayer prepares you to more fully participate in the Mass and receive the Eucharist worthily. In daily prayer you learn to turn aside from distractions and focus your mind and heart on Christ.

7. Prayer leads to divine union. God desires you to reach union with him, being completely obedient to his will and loving him with your whole heart, mind, soul, and strength.[8] You were created for this very purpose. Such union is impossible without prayer.

The Catechism sums it up this way: "The living and true God tirelessly calls each person to that mysterious encounter known as prayer."[9] See also the book *Mental Prayer: The*

---

[7] Saint John Chrysostom *De Anna* 4, 5.
[8] See Dt 6:5.
[9] CCC no. 2567.

Great Means of Salvation and of Perfection by Saint Alphonsus Liguori, especially chapter 1.

4. *What are the forms of Christian prayer?*

The Catechism[10] tells us that Christians have practiced many forms of prayer throughout the centuries, including:

- Blessing and Adoration
- Petition
- Intercession
- Thanksgiving
- Praise

These forms speak about the content of prayer, *what* you pray. You can offer each of these prayers alone or in the liturgy and other communal settings.

5. *What are the three expressions of personal prayer?*

The Catechism notes three *expressions* of personal prayer.[11] They explain *how* you pray:

- Vocal Prayer
- Meditation
- Contemplative Prayer

These are broad categories of prayer, rather than specific methods. Vocal prayer is the most basic of personal prayers. As your faith matures, you should add meditation to your prayer practice. Eventually, if you are faithful to prayer and

---

[10] CCC nos. 2626-2643.
[11] Ibid. nos. 2700-2719.

obedient to God and the Church, God may grant you the gift of contemplative prayer.

Vocal prayer, prayed well, blends into meditation. Meditation prayed well prepares a soul for the gift of infused contemplation.[12] Infused contemplation is a mysterious communion with God. It is the prayer of saints. It is also what God desires for you. The Catechism says about meditation, "This form of prayerful reflection is of great value, but Christian prayer should go further: to the knowledge of the love of the Lord Jesus, to union with him."[13] Christian prayer "should go ... to union with him." All truly Christian prayer tends toward this union with Jesus. Union is accomplished in contemplation.

6. What is vocal prayer?

Vocal prayer is pre-composed, usually by someone else. The first prayers you learned as a child, such as the Hail Mary, the Guardian Angel Prayer, and Grace before meals, are vocal prayers. Vocal prayers are designed to be prayed in communal settings, which implies saying them aloud. That's why they have traditionally been called *vocal.* However, the term *vocal prayer* refers to this most basic level (or grade) of prayer, whether prayed aloud or silently.

---

[12] The Catechism uses the term *contemplative prayer* rather than *contemplation*. Numbers 2709-10 speak of contemplative prayer as something active, at least at times. The remainder of the section corresponds to what the doctors of the Church teach about infused contemplation.

[13] CCC no. 2708.

7. What is meditation?

The word *meditation* has many meanings. The basic dictionary meaning of meditation is *pondering*. Christian meditation involves thinking about some truth of the Faith, then
using your thoughts to move you toward conversation with
God. The Catechism says,

> "Meditation engages thought, imagination, emotion,
> and desire. This ... is necessary in order to deepen
> our convictions of faith, prompt the conversion of
> our heart, and strengthen our will to follow Christ.
> Christian prayer tries above all to meditate on the
> mysteries of Christ, as in *lectio divina* or the ro-
> sary."[14]

Meditation is not a particular method of prayer; the Catechism notes that there are numerous different methods of
meditation you can use.[15] The particular method you choose
is less important than engaging your mind, heart, and imagination in drawing close to God and speaking to him.

For more on this subject, see the section **Meditation:
Christian Versus Non-Christian.**

8. What is contemplation?

According to Saint Teresa of Ávila and Saint John of the
Cross, who are doctors of the Church because of their teaching on contemplation, contemplation is an experiential,
"loving knowledge"[16] of God that cannot be produced by

---

[14] CCC no. 2708.
[15] Ibid. no. 2707.
[16] This is a term used by St. John of the Cross throughout his
works.

human action. It is infused into the soul by God himself. Contemplation is a conversation with God that goes beyond words, images, and concepts. It is a loving gaze between God and the soul.

In the beginning of the life of prayer, the activity of the soul predominates. Discursive meditation, affective prayer, and acquired recollection are all grades of active prayer (see **Question 82**). These are prayers you can make by your efforts, aided with common actual grace. In order to keep growing in prayer from one stage to the next, you need to surrender more and more of your life to God. This surrender, along with prayer, prepares you for a deeper union with God. For most people, the process of surrender takes years.

Contemplation begins when God initiates a loving conversation with you that is beyond words. In contemplation, he draws you into a deeper union with himself. It is not something you can practice; you can only prepare for it. The initial experiences of contemplation are sometimes so subtle that you may not even recognize them. Little by little, however, you find yourself unable to practice the active prayer forms. God's work is now predominating and your role is to quietly receive what he offers.

Teresa of Ávila spoke about different stages of prayer as four different ways of watering a garden (see **Question 85**). For clarity and brevity, we can simplify them to two here. Meditation is like drawing water up from a well — lots of work. Contemplation is like rain on the garden — beyond your control. All you can do is prepare the garden and then receive the rain.

Mental Prayer and Meditation

9. *What is mental prayer?*

The Catechism does not list mental prayer as one of the three expressions of personal prayer (see **Question 5**), but the term *mental prayer* has been used by Catholics for centuries. Saint Teresa of Ávila says:

> Mental prayer, in my opinion, is nothing else than a close sharing between friends; it means taking time frequently to be alone with him who we know loves us.[17]

Teresa sees two aspects to mental prayer: sharing with a friend (remembering that this Friend is far above you, but nevertheless calls you into an intimate relationship with himself); and time set aside specifically to be alone with God. The word *mental* signifies that this prayer comes from your own mind, rather than being written down by someone else, as in vocal prayer. It is usually a silent prayer, but does not always have to be (see **Question 11**). When you spend time with a friend, you do not usually recite to him or her someone else's words about friendship. When you spend

---

[17] *The Book of Her Life* 8, 5. *Collected Works of St. Teresa of Ávila*, translated by Kieran Kavanaugh, OCD, and Otilio Rodriguez, OCD (Washington, DC: ICS, 1976), Vol. 1, 96.

time with a spouse, you don't usually read Shakespeare's sonnets to that person. Instead, you speak from the heart. You know you can share your deepest self with your companion, because you love one another and will not reject each other. The time you spend together draws you even closer.

Some authors include both meditation and contemplation in the term *mental prayer,* which is the way it is used in this book.[18] Other authors use the term *mental prayer* as a synonym for *meditation.*

Since mental prayer is a *sharing,* you should expect God to reveal himself in some way to you as well. In fact. John of the Cross said that all true prayer brings an increase in knowledge of God. In meditation, God primarily reveals himself through Scripture and the truths of the Faith. In contemplation, he gives an experiential knowledge of himself that you cannot put into words.[19]

---

[18] Calling both meditation and contemplation *mental prayer* can remind you that whether or not you experience contemplation in any specific prayer time is up to God. You sit down for mental prayer, attempt to practice meditation, then allow the Holy Spirit to break in as he wills. The doctors of the Church teach that in the higher levels of contemplation, meditation becomes and stays impossible, so that you no longer need to attempt to meditate. However, contemplation must still be received as a pure gift, not as something owed or taken for granted. Continuing to call your prayer time *mental prayer* can also preserve the humility and hiddenness that is necessary for contemplation to flourish. In other words, saying, "I've got to go do my contemplation," sounds as though you are in control, not the Holy Spirit. It also reveals to listeners, perhaps unnecessarily, that you have advanced in prayer beyond the common experience.

[19] *The Ascent of Mt. Carmel* 2, 14. When you are going through the passive nights (see Question 93), it may seem that God is absent, so that the sharing aspect of prayer is not apparent. However,

10. Is mental prayer more effective than vocal prayer?

Mental prayer is a higher grade (or level) of prayer than vocal prayer (see **Question 82**). Most people will learn vocal prayer first and then gradually begin praying mental prayer.

It is better to pray vocal prayer well than to pray mental prayer carelessly. However, all things being equal, mental prayer does in itself have a greater potential to move the mind and heart toward God. It is more likely to bring you to greater intimacy with God. It is also more likely that those who practice mental prayer will say their vocal prayers well. Saint Alphonsus Liguori writes:

> In general, vocal prayers are said distractedly with the voice of the body, but not the heart, especially when they are long, and still more especially when said by a person who does not make mental prayer; and therefore, God seldom hears them, and seldom grants the graces asked.[20]

Mental prayer done well transforms you. It brings you toward complete conversion.[21] Due to this transforming effect, those who practice mental prayer will generally have more efficacious prayer, whether they are engaged in mental prayer itself or in vocal prayer. Likewise, those who have advanced to the level of contemplative prayer, since they

---

God is actually sharing himself with you in a deeper way; you are just not yet ready to perceive his presence.

[20] *Mental Prayer: The Great Means of Salvation and of Perfection* Chap. 1. https://www.ourcatholicprayers.com/alphonsus-liguori-on-mental-prayer.html.

[21] Ibid. Chap. 2.

enjoy a greater union with God, pray more efficaciously than those who have not experienced contemplation. This efficacy will extend toward all the prayers they offer to God.

11. Can I pray mental prayer aloud?

Silence is a vital part of prayer. In order to experience deeper forms of prayer, you must learn to be quiet (see **Question 43**). The term *mental* implies thought, while the term *vocal* implies speech. However, some people prefer to read aloud the Scripture passage they are meditating on before entering into silence. Reading aloud helps them to overcome distractions at the beginning of prayer. This is perfectly acceptable. It is also acceptable to pray aloud when you are particularly tired or suffering from brain fog. Your prayer remains mental prayer, even though you are speaking. On the other hand, you should do your best to include some silence in every mental prayer time. God will more likely act when you are silent and attentive to him.

12. Is mental prayer the same thing as meditation?

Mental prayer includes all prayer in which you set aside time for heart-to-heart conversation with God. This could include any of the forms of Christian prayer when prayed in your own words (see **Question 4**). However, meditation is the Church's preferred and recommended form of mental prayer. As **Question 5** stated, the Catechism lists the three expressions of personal prayer as vocal prayer, meditation, and contemplative prayer. When the saints speak of *practicing* mental prayer, they are generally referring to meditation. When they speak of mental prayer in general, you must look at the context to understand whether they are speaking specifically about meditation or contemplation or both.

13. Is praying spontaneously throughout the day a form of mental prayer?

While the spontaneous prayers you say throughout the day truly are a means of speaking to God from the heart, *mental prayer* refers most specifically to time set aside to be alone with God. Keeping this distinction emphasizes the necessity of spending time alone with God daily. Praying while engaged in other activities is a supplement to mental prayer, not a substitute. Saint Alphonsus Liguori implies that this is true when, in his book on praying throughout the day, he tells readers to start their day with mental prayer.[22]

14. Is meditation the same as Bible study?

Bible study is a wonderful pastime that enriches your faith and can enrich your prayer. But Bible study — in the sense of looking up word meanings, consulting maps, or digging into Bible history — should generally be separate from mental prayer. In mental prayer, you read Scripture not in order to know facts, but in order to fall in love with the God who is love.

The Congregation for the Doctrine of the Faith (CDF) has called prayer "a personal, intimate and profound dialogue

---

[22] St. Alphonsus Liguori, *How to Pray at All Times* Chap. 5, https://www.ecatholic2000.com/cts/untitled-211.shtml. Accessed 5/29/19.

between man and God."[23] Reading Scripture during prayer is not only a preparation for that dialog, it is part of it.

When you sit down to pray, one of the first things you should do is ask the Holy Spirit to speak to your heart through the Scriptures. Then when you read, you do so slowly, with attention. You engage your mind and heart with the text — not so much to understand the Faith better, but to get to know Jesus better, and to discern what difference his life and teaching make to your relationship with God.

15. Can I practice both meditative and Charismatic prayer?

Charismatic prayer could refer to praise and worship, as in the singing or adoring of God with raised hands. Praise and worship would be akin to the stage of meditation called affective prayer, in which your heart is moved to speak lovingly to God (see **Question 84**). Another type of prayer typically prayed by Charismatics is speaking in tongues. In this gift of the Holy Spirit, you speak to God in a "tongue of men or of angels" (1 Cor 13:1), without understanding the words. Both of these forms of prayer may be used outside your mental prayer time, especially at prayer meetings. These practices would not hinder you from meditation on Scripture.

What about praying in these ways during your mental prayer time? If you as a Charismatic begin by prayerfully

---

[23] *On Some Aspects of Christian Meditation* no. 3., October 15, 1989. http://www.vatican.va/roman_curia/congregations/cfaith/docume nts/rc_con_cfaith_doc_19891015_meditazione-cristiana_en.html. Accessed 5/29/19.

reading Scripture and feel moved toward either praise and worship or speaking in tongues, you may follow that impulse. You should not purposely practice Charismatic prayer *in place of* your meditation, however. Meditation has the unique ability to teach you to know and love Christ better, which is why it is universally recommended by the saints. Focusing exclusively on Charismatic types of prayer can make you attached to the consolations those practices bring. Saint John of the Cross would caution you not to take delight in Charismatic experiences themselves, but use them to build up the Church, as that is what Charismatic gifts are intended for. [24]

16. Are vocal prayer and mental prayer mutually exclusive?

Like mental prayer, vocal prayer is meant to move you forward in your relationship with God. At first, vocal prayer might be little more than rote. As you come to understand the words better and grow in your relationship with God, you begin to pray even your vocal prayers from the heart. They are no longer just the words of an unknown writer; they are an expression of what you yourself would like to say to the Lord. Saint Teresa says that when you pray vocal prayer with loving, reverent attention it, in fact, becomes mental prayer.[25]

---

[24] For an extended exploration of John of the Cross' teaching on the Charismatic gifts, see Dr. Ralph Martin's essay, *Charismatic and Contemplative: What Would John of the Cross Say?* https://www.renewalministries.net/?module=Page&sID=free-literature. Accessed 5/29/19.

[25] *Interior Castle* 1, 1.

There are also vocal prayers that have meditation built into them, most notably the Rosary. You can focus simply on the words of the prayer, but meditating on the mysteries often helps you go deeper.

On the subject of vocal prayer blending into mental prayer, Saint Francis de Sales advises:

> If, while saying vocal prayers, your heart feels drawn to mental prayer, do not resist it, but calmly let your mind fall into that channel, without troubling because you have not finished your appointed vocal prayers. The mental prayer you have substituted for them is more acceptable to God, and more profitable to your soul. I should make an exception of the Church's Offices [the Liturgy of the Hours], if you are bound to say those by your vocation — in such a case they are your duty.[26]

Beginning vocal prayer and moving into mental prayer is therefore a positive development. And sometimes when your mental prayer is particularly distracted or you are fatigued, you can draw on vocal prayer to help you.

For more on this subject, see the book I co-wrote with Dan Burke, *The Contemplative Rosary.*[27]

---

[26] *Introduction to the Devout Life* 2, 1. https://www.ourcatholicprayers.com/saint-francis-de-sales-on-mental-prayer.html.

[27] Available at major online bookstores and your local Catholic bookstore, or at EWTNrc.com.

17. Why is meditation important?

The Catechism states:

> The Church "forcefully and specially exhorts all the Christian faithful ... to learn 'the surpassing knowledge of Jesus Christ' (Phil 3:8) by frequent reading of the divine Scriptures.... Let them remember, however, that prayer should accompany the reading of Sacred Scripture, so that a dialogue takes place between God and man. For 'we speak to him when we pray; we listen to him when we read the divine oracles.'"[28]

Notice that the Church is not *suggesting* Catholics read and pray over Scripture, nor even *encouraging* them to do so. Instead, she is *forcefully and specially exhorting* (i.e., *urging*) them. Why so strong a statement?

Meditating on Scripture makes mental prayer a true dialog between God and man. Scripture is the publicly revealed Word of God. It is a trustworthy teacher concerning God and his will. When you read the Scriptures in prayer, God speaks directly to you. You can ask yourself, "What does the Holy Spirit want me to glean from this passage? What is he teaching me about the character of God? How do I fall short in following what he teaches? How does God require me to change?"

The Catechism goes on to say:

> To meditate on what we read helps us to make it our own by confronting it with ourselves. Here, another book is opened: the book of life. We pass from

---

[28] CCC no. 2653, citing *Dei Verbum* 25.

thoughts to reality. To the extent that we are humble and faithful, we discover in meditation the movements that stir the heart and we are able to discern them. It is a question of acting truthfully in order to come into the light: 'Lord, what do you want me to do?'[29]

Many Catholics miss an essential point regarding meditation: Christian meditation is beloved by the Church because it moves you to conversion. You compare the ideal expressed in the Gospels with the concrete details of your life. Scripture acts as an examination of conscience. It shows you where you fall short, but also encourages you with the love of God and the example of the saints of old. It urges you to open your heart to the grace of the Holy Spirit.

Few other types of mental prayer provide this benefit. You can easily make your prayer time focused on your needs and desires, rather than on God's desires for you. Meditating on Scripture keeps God, not self, at the center of prayer.

18. If I can only do mental prayer or go to daily Mass, which should I choose?

If you are able to do both, do both. Objectively speaking, the Mass is a higher prayer than your mental prayer. In the Mass, the sacrifice of Christ is offered to the Father. Jesus said that without the Eucharist, you will not have life within you.[30] The more often you can receive him, or just be in his presence, the better.

---

[29] Ibid. no. 2706.
[30] Jn 6:53.

However, for various reasons — including demanding jobs, having young children, poor health, age, and distance from the nearest church — many people simply cannot attend Mass daily. You should not fail in your duties of your vocation because you choose to go to daily Mass.

In contrast, all but a very few people can practice mental prayer daily. Mental prayer does not require health or travel. You can pray in the middle of the night, while the kids are napping, or on your lunch break at work. (See **Question 23** for more ideas on how to find time to pray.) For these reasons, the better choice for many lay people will be mental prayer.

In order to fully receive the graces God offers you in the Eucharist, you must have the right disposition. It is nearly impossible to cultivate this disposition without daily mental prayer. As you commit yourself to praying daily, you will surrender your heart more and more to God. You will come to love and desire the Eucharist, reverence it, and be more recollected throughout the entire Mass, as your prayer deepens. Thus, through mental prayer, you are much better prepared for Sunday Mass than you would be by going to daily Mass without mental prayer or the proper recollection for Mass.

If you cannot attend daily Mass, it may help to recall that in former eras the faithful did not receive the Eucharist regularly, even when they attended Mass. Yet many became saints. Also, you may make a daily spiritual communion a part of your routine, which will increase your desire to receive the Blessed Sacrament even more.

Of course, if daily Mass is workable for you, you should make use of this great grace. Try to slip in a few minutes of mental prayer before Mass in order to prepare yourself properly, especially if you are not doing mental prayer at other times.

The Council of Trent taught about the Holy Eucharist:

> Now as to the use of this holy sacrament, our Fathers have rightly and wisely distinguished three ways of receiving it. For they have taught that some receive it [1] sacramentally only, to wit sinners: [2] others spiritually only, those to wit who eating in desire that heavenly bread which is set before them, are, by a lively faith which worketh by charity, made sensible of the fruit and usefulness thereof: whereas the third (class) [3] receive it both sacramentally and spiritually, and these are they who so prove and prepare themselves beforehand, as to approach to this divine table clothed with the wedding garment.[31]

Case 2 describes what happens when you practice a spiritual communion at home without going to Mass. It is definitely more efficacious for your relationship with God than case 1, receiving without the proper disposition. Ideally, you should become the person described in case 3, attending Mass with the proper disposition.

If you can truly do only one or the other, you may want to speak to a spiritual director before you decide which is best for you at this time. Either way, make sure that when your circumstances change, you do both.

---

[31] First Decree, Chap. VIII.

19. If I pray the Rosary daily, why do I still have to pray mental prayer?

The Rosary is an example of vocal prayer, but it is a vocal prayer that has a unique ability to become mental prayer. When you pray the Rosary, you are meant to meditate upon the mysteries, just as you meditate on Scripture in mental prayer. Of course, you do not usually address the Lord in your own words following the Rosary meditations; rather, you let the prayers of the Rosary themselves express what is in your heart.

Saint Teresa speaks of the importance of thinking reverently and lovingly about God in all your vocal prayers. Doing so can transform them into mental prayer.

> You are right in saying that this vocal prayer is now in fact mental prayer. But I tell you that surely I don't know how mental prayer can be separated from vocal prayer if the vocal prayer is to be recited well with the understanding of whom we are speaking to. It is even an obligation that we strive to pray with attention.[32]

So, then, is the Rosary "enough?" There are two potential problems with this question. The first concerns your motive for asking it. The phrase "do I have to" often betrays a spiritual minimalism that earlier Christian authors would have identified as the sin of *acedia*.[33] If you are only con-

---

[32] *The Way of Perfection* Chap. 24.
[33] Acedia is a sin that is often wrongly identified with laziness. It goes much deeper than that, to the very heart of the spiritual life. Acedia is a manifestation of putting other things before God. For an excellent explanation of what acedia entails and how it has

cerned with what you "have" to do, your spiritual life will stagnate before you advance very far. Recall the rich young man, who asked Jesus, "Teacher, what good deed must I do, to have eternal life" (Mt 19:16)? Jesus' answer was to keep the commandments. Well, the young man had done that. So it appears he had done what he "had to." Jesus wasn't finished with him, however.

> Jesus said to him, "If you would be perfect, go, sell what you possess and give to the poor, and you will have treasure in heaven; and come, follow me." When the young man heard this he went away sorrowful; for he had great possessions.[34]

The young man wasn't lacking what was strictly necessary for salvation; he was lacking what was necessary for perfection. Yet, what happened? Instead of following Jesus, "he went away." Then Jesus spoke to his disciples about the difficulty of getting to heaven when one is rich. Apparently, even though this man had done what was generally required, his unwillingness to do something more than that endangered his salvation.

When you truly love God, you are not concerned with where the line lies between the necessary and the optional. You desire to do all you can ("sell all you have") to come closer to him. If the thought of practicing mental prayer makes you feel sad or despairing, you are probably falling prey to acedia. Remember, God never asks anything of you

---

become a plague in the modern age, see *The Noonday Devil: Acedia, the Unnamed Evil of Our Times* by Dom Jean-Charles Nault, OSB.

[34] Mt 19:21-22.

without giving you the grace to obey. Spend some time praying and examining your conscience on this point.

The second potential problem with this question is that few people plumb the depths of the Rosary in a way that makes it a good stand-in for mental prayer. In fact, those who practice mental prayer regularly are much more likely to find their vocal prayers fruitful (see **Question 10**). It is extremely easy to let the Rosary fall into a simple rote prayer. It's much harder for mental prayer to become rote, when you have to speak with God in your own words.

Saint Francis de Sales wrote,

> It is well, too, to say pious Litanies, and the other vocal prayers appointed for the Hours and found in the Manual of devotion, — but if you have a gift for mental prayer, let that always take the chief place, so that if, having made that, you are hindered by business or any other cause from saying your wonted [usual] vocal prayer, do not be disturbed. ...[35]

Make mental prayer the top priority in your pray routine, while continuing to pray the Rosary as well, if possible. If you can only practice one or the other, make it mental prayer.

20. What if I miss my mental prayer time?

Saint Francis de Sales answers this question as follows:

> If you are unable all day to make up for the omission, you must remedy it as far as may be by ejaculatory prayer, and by reading some spiritual book, to-

---

[35] *Introduction to the Devout Life* 2, 1.

gether with an act of penitence for the neglect, together with a steadfast resolution to do better the
next day.[36]

In other words, do your best not to miss mental prayer.
But if you ever should, then make sure you pray throughout
the day, offering little words of praise to God. You may not
have time to do spiritual reading if you do not have time to
make up your mental prayer later in the day, but you should
be able to give something up as reparation. Go without des-
sert, pray your vocal prayers on your knees, do an extra
kind act for a family member, et cetera. These acts take lit-
tle-to-no extra time and help make up for the prayer you
have missed.

---

[36] Ibid.

Conditions for Prayer

21. How do I begin a life of prayer?

Start by praying your vocal prayer as well as you can. It is more important to pray well at the stage where you are than to try and advance quickly to higher states of prayer. Say all your prayers, even the Sign of the Cross, with reverence, love, and attention to Jesus. Avoid mortal sin and its near occasion and begin going to Confession more often. Soon you will desire to speak with God from the heart (that is, practice mental prayer). Mental prayer is the next step.

22. How can I establish a prayer habit?

The first step in establishing a habit of prayer is making prayer your top priority. Yes, top. Put it above family obligations, work, rest, or anything else.[37] When Martha complained to Jesus that her sister Mary was sitting at his feet while Martha handled all the dinner preparations, Jesus said Mary was occupied with "the one thing necessary" (Lk 10:38-42). Mary, engaged in listening to Jesus, shows the importance of spending time in mental prayer.

---

[37] Of course, this excludes the Sunday Mass obligation. See Question 18 on whether to choose daily Mass or mental prayer.

Prayer does not conflict with your duties; it supports them. Of course, it's possible to overdo it, spending time at Adoration, for example, when the kids need a bath, the house is a mess, and it's past time for dinner. But in our culture, most people err in the other direction, thinking that they cannot possibly pray when they have so many duties.

If you put off mental prayer until a later day when you have more time, will that day ever come? Won't you be more likely to spend your free time later with something else? God wants your heart now. He works in the present. If you give him the little time you have, he will bless it and provide you with more.

Here are three ways to make it easier to form the habit of prayer:

1. Pray at the same time each day. Write it into your schedule if necessary.

2. Pray in the same place each day. Many people set up a home altar or a special room for prayer.

3. Set aside distractions. That may mean changing your routine or having a calming activity as a transition between every-day life and prayer.[38] Some example activities might be a few minutes of spiritual reading, listening to sacred music, doing a crossword puzzle, or taking a short walk.

---

[38] Author Dan Burke calls these three items sacred time, sacred space, and sacred attention. See his excellent introduction to meditation, *Into the Deep: Finding Peace through Prayer.*

23. How can I find time to pray?

Where is the time for prayer to come from? Here are several suggestions.

Making the time for prayer requires sacrifice. It could come in the realm of entertainment. Consider how much time you spend watching movies and TV. Could you skip half an hour's program daily and spend the time with God instead?

The more technology our culture has, the busier people seem to be. No one has time to just sit any more. In order to make the time to sit and talk to God, you may have to simplify your life. Can you take a fast from Facebook? Could you limit the activities your kids need a chauffeur for? Or say *no* to the next volunteer opportunity?

Simplifying your life sometimes extends to material possessions. The more you possess, the more time you will need to spend on the upkeep of your possessions. How much time could you save if you had a smaller house? Gave your surplus goods to the poor? Took vacations closer to home? Minimized your cell phone data plan?

Your whole family may need to make adjustments so you can all become more prayerful. Busy parents may need their spouse or older children to help them find time for prayer. Can you do tag-team mental prayer in the evenings and on weekends? Put a sibling in charge of little ones? Make use of a toddler's nap time? Pray while nursing the baby?

How about visiting an Adoration chapel during your lunch break or just before or after work? Or simply praying in your office or car? Working closer to home so your commute is shorter? Making simpler meals? Assigning more chores to the kids? Being satisfied with a slightly messy house?

Each person will answer these questions differently, but no one establishes a prayer life without sacrifice in one area or another. This sacrifice will help you form the habit of detachment that is necessary for prayer growth.

24. What's the best time for prayer?

Your best time for prayer may be that half hour when you reflexively hit the snooze button. You aren't being productive then anyway, and you're not getting much rest. If you can, schedule prayer for the first thing in the morning. You're less likely to forget it or let other activities take priority. Saint Francis de Sales says:

> Give an hour every day to meditation before dinner [that is, lunch]; — if you can, let it be early in the morning, when your mind will be less cumbered, and fresh after the night's rest.[39]

Praying before rather than after major meals will make falling asleep less likely.

The best time to pray, however, is the time when you tend to be most awake, least distracted, and consistent. First thing in the morning is the best time in general, but it will not work with everyone's schedule. If you need to, experiment to see what time works best for you. Then be consistent with it.

---

[39] *Introduction to the Devout Life* 2, 1.

25. What's the best place for prayer?

Saint Francis de Sales counsels lay people:

> If you can make your meditation quietly in church, it will be well, and no one, father or mother, husband or wife, can object to an hour spent there, and very probably you could not secure a time so free from interruption at home.[40]

As in previous questions, there is an ideal, and then there is what practically works for you. Few lay people with families today can do their daily mental prayer in a church, but many can go to Adoration once a week. A good substitute is a place at home specifically set aside for prayer and set up as an altar of sorts. Even this is not strictly necessary, however, nor always possible. At the least, find a place that is usually quiet and where you can close the door to separate yourself from family members. Don't pray in a place where you are likely to be distracted by tasks that need to get done, such as in an office or kitchen, unless you have no better option. Find silence and solitude the best that you can and then stick with the same place and time, so that you are more psychologically prepared to pray, out of force of habit.

26. What's the best posture for praying?

The best posture for prayer is the one which least distracts you and most helps you pray. Lying in bed when you are physically well is generally a bad idea. It doesn't show reverence for God and it's liable to end in sleep. At the opposite

---

[40] Ibid.

end of the spectrum, kneeling is respectful, but may result in your thinking about how uncomfortable you are, rather than how good God is. Sitting comfortably rests in the middle. It's a position nearly everyone can take and it doesn't require extra effort.

Occasionally you may find taking a "prayer walk" helpful, especially when you are sleepy or cannot find a quiet spot at home to pray. For most people, however, walking is best restricted to extraordinary times, as it does not lend itself to meditation on Scripture.

Some people put too much emphasis on prayer positions. You will find many articles on prayer beginning with instructions such as, "Sit with your back straight and your feet flat on the floor." Others will tell you not to move at all during prayer. These strictures make prayer less natural, rather than more so. God is not concerned over whether your back is perfectly straight while you pray. Neither does refusing to shift when you are uncomfortable make you less distracted by your body. Let your body work for you, rather than hinder you.

27. How long should I pray each day?

This is a complex question. The answer depends on where you are in your spiritual life, as well as your vocation and life circumstances.

For someone who is just starting to devote daily time to conversation with God, any time spent in mental prayer is better than none. You do want to make it meaningful, however, spending enough time so that you can progress in union with God.

Fifteen minutes is a reasonable goal for most lay people who are just starting out. Sometimes with lots of distractions, a fifteen-minute prayer time might yield only a few minutes of heartfelt prayer. It might take five minutes just to set aside your other thoughts so that you can begin to focus on God. You do not want to stop when your prayer is really just beginning. But if you cannot manage praying for fifteen minutes, pray for ten. If you cannot manage ten minutes, pray for five. Any heartfelt prayer is better than none.

What about people who have already been praying for some time? If you can manage to pray a bit longer without compromising your duties, do so. Saint Francis de Sales counseled lay people not to spend more than an hour in mental prayer, unless advised to do so by their spiritual director.[41] Any more than this and your job or family is likely to suffer. Of course, a retired couple may have many more hours free than a family with young children or a working spouse.

Once you have set a time goal, stick to it. Be generous with God, but also be reasonable. If you expect yourself to pray as long as a saint from day one, you are likely succumbing to pride. You are also likely setting yourself up for failure. Many saints have said that it is better to pray a little and consistently each day than to pray for hours one day and none the next. Do what you can, and when you feel moved to expand your prayer time, do so slowly.

28. What are the immediate preparations for mental prayer?

Saints speak about placing yourself in the presence of God at the beginning of prayer. This can mean thinking about

---

[41] Introduction to the Devout Life 2, 1.

God's presence within your soul. You can also picture yourself being surrounded by God. Or you could call up a mental image, such as the Crucifixion. You may try picturing yourself setting your cares at the feet of Jesus as a way of setting aside your distractions. Practices such as focusing on your breath can be of help to some, especially if your mind is racing or you are feeling anxious. However, people often overemphasize the need for and efficacy of these physical practices. If you use them, make sure you move on to actual prayer as soon as possible, so you do not mistake any peaceful feelings these purely natural techniques give you for closeness to God. Prayer does not consist in physical or mental exercises.

When you have placed yourself in God's presence, call on the Holy Spirit to guide your prayer. Usually this brief preparation will be enough to at least begin prayer focused on God.

Saint Francis de Sales counsels regarding another preparation for prayer:

> If it should happen that your morning goes by without the usual meditation, either owing to a pressure of business, or from any other cause, (which interruptions you should try to prevent as far as possible,) try to repair the loss in the afternoon, but not immediately after a meal, or you will perhaps be drowsy, which is bad both for your meditation and your health.[42]

---

[42] Ibid.

Eating a big meal just before mental prayer will often result in sleeping through prayer. See **Questions 65 and 66** for more on this aspect of preparation for prayer.

29. What lifestyle best supports mental prayer?

Prayer is affected by the way you live the rest of your life. The best support for mental prayer is frequent reception of the sacraments. Striving to live a virtuous life is absolutely necessary for growth in prayer. This includes working on conquering deliberate sin.

You can also support your prayer life by regulating the activities throughout your day that are likely to distract you when you come to prayer. Some examples may be using the TV or radio as constant background noise, watching fast-paced movies, or binging on digital media.

Working on detachment also boosts prayer (see **Questions 31-33**). Most distractions in prayer result from inordinate attachments to something other than God. Other distractions come from a lack of trust in God, which leads to worry. The more you put God first, the easier prayer becomes.[43]

30. How is virtue related to prayer?

Teresa of Ávila's constant teaching is that prayer cannot grow unless you are also striving to live a virtuous life. Conversely, a virtuous life finds its strength in prayer. In the

---

[43] Of course, desolation in prayer comes and goes (see Question 50), and everyone who continues to grow will eventually experience the difficult prayer known as the passive nights. See the section Difficulties in Meditation for more on these and other problems that can continue to make prayer hard.

midst of a book for her nuns on prayer, she makes a segue to speak of virtue. Then she explains herself:

> You will ask, my daughters, why I am talking to you about virtues when you have more than enough books to teach you about them and when you want me to tell you only about contemplation. My reply is that, if you had asked me about meditation, I could have talked to you about it, and advised you all to practise it, even if you do not possess the virtues. For this is the first step to be taken toward the acquisition of the virtues and the very life of all Christians depends upon their beginning it. No one, however lost a soul he may be, should neglect so great a blessing if God inspires him to make use of it. All this I have already written elsewhere, and so have many others who know what they are writing about, which I certainly do not: God knows that. But contemplation, daughters, is another matter.[44]

In other words, anyone can start a life of prayer. You do not have to be a saint to begin practicing mental prayer. It is mental prayer that will sanctify you. However, if you wish to advance in prayer to reach contemplation, you must practice virtue.

The Congregation for the Doctrine of the Faith also addressed this question:

> The seeking of God through prayer has to be preceded and accompanied by an ascetical struggle and a purification from one's own sins and errors, since

---

[44] *The Way of Perfection* Chap.16.

Jesus has said that only "the pure of heart shall see God" (Mt 5:8). The Gospel aims above all at a moral purification from the lack of truth and love and, on a deeper level, from all the selfish instincts which impede man from recognizing and accepting the Will of God in its purity.[45]

It may seem that the CDF is contradicting Teresa here by saying that purification must precede prayer, but there is a sense in which even your first prayer time must be at least accompanied by mortification. You have to make the sacrifice of your time, which you could be spending on something other than prayer. As your prayer grows, not only your virtue, but also your practices of mortification ("ascetical struggle") must deepen. (See **Questions 97 and 98**.)

31. What is detachment?

Detachment in Catholic spirituality refers to being free from disordered attachments. *Disordered* literally means *out of order*. When your life is rightly ordered, you have the correct priorities. God comes first. Everything and everyone else receives attention in accordance with his will. Conversely, a disordered life means you have made things or people into little idols, putting them ahead of God. You might use food, digital devices, or money in a way that does not honor God.

Christian detachment is different from Buddhist detachment. Buddhists take a step back from everything — including their own thoughts and feelings, and ultimately

---

[45] *On Some Aspects of Christian Meditation* no. 18. Capitalization as in the original.

their own self — because they believe everything is transitory and more or less an illusion. Their goal is freedom from suffering, and attachments are seen to cause suffering. In Buddhism all attachments are ultimately bad.

In Christianity, some attachments, such as to family and friends, are good, as long as they align with God's will. Christian detachment does not mean being cold-hearted. It fulfills the greatest commandment: "You shall love the Lord your God with all your heart, and with all your soul, and with all your mind."[46] The more you love God, the easier it is to love your neighbor and to use material goods for God's glory. With respect to other people, Christian detachment means willing God's will for them, instead of your own. It means seeing the image of God in them and treating them with the respect that image demands. A truly detached person never uses others for his own ends. Since he obeys the greatest commandment, he is also able to obey the second: "You shall love your neighbor as yourself."[47] If you are married, perhaps with children, God wills for you to love your spouse and kids. In fact, as you grow closer to God, you will love them more truly, because you will be less selfish and more understanding. You will serve them without seeking anything for yourself in return.

Detachment brings freedom, freedom to love God and others without selfish clinging getting in your way. It also enables you to pray more deeply. The less you are attached to pleasures, the less they will distract you during prayer.

---

[46] Mt 22:37.
[47] Mt 22:39.

32. Why is detachment necessary?

Jesus said, "So therefore, whoever of you does not renounce all he has cannot be my disciple."[48] The Catechism, basing its teaching on these words of Christ, says, "The precept of detachment from riches is obligatory for entrance into the Kingdom of heaven."[49] Attachments keep you from seeing God face to face. If you are inordinately attached to anything or anyone, you have not followed the greatest commandment (see **Question 31**). Being purged from your attachments is not optional. If you do not overcome them on earth, you will need to be cleansed from them in Purgatory.[50]

Detachment has benefits for this life as well. Saint John of the Cross wrote, "The Soul that desires God to surrender Himself to it entirely must surrender itself entirely to Him without keeping anything for itself."[51] When you keep God at arm's length (or even at finger's length) he cannot unite you with himself.

To use another metaphor, if your soul is full of earthly things, you leave no room for God. Consuming spiritual junk food leaves no room for what will really nourish you. Only God can satisfy your desires. Only God can give you true happiness. The more you seek happiness through other people and material things, the less happy you will be. You were made for union with God. Nothing less will suffice.

Attachments also cloud your vision. Jesus instructed his disciples to remove the plank from their eye in order to see

---

[48] Lk 14:33.
[49] CCC no. 2544.
[50] Ibid. no. 1030.
[51] *Sayings of Light and Love* 128.

clearly. That plank is often sin, but it can also be a disordered attachment. Attachments jeopardize your ability to give good advice and real help to other people.[52]

33. How can I practice detachment?

Christian detachment is rooted in love. The more you love God, the more you will order your life in accordance with his will. Think of it this way. When you fall in love with someone, everyone and everything else in your life pales beside your beloved. You change your schedule and your priorities. You spend money and time on that person without feeling like it's a sacrifice. The same is true in your relationship with God.

One of the best ways to begin on the road of detachment, therefore, is forming a habit of meditating on Scripture. In meditation, you learn about the character of God and let this knowledge affect your life. You begin to fall in love with Jesus. Little by little, the activities you used to engage in that were not in accordance with his will lose their hold on you. You also learn to follow the Lord's example of detachment.[53]

This process begins with mortal sin, then venial sin, and finally disordered attachments that may not themselves be sinful. In other words, start with the biggest things, those things that are hindering your spiritual growth the most. It doesn't make sense to focus on overcoming an attachment

---

[52] See Mt 7:3-5.
[53] See Fr. Gabriel of St. Mary Magdalene, OCD, *Union with God According to St. John of the Cross* (Eugene, OR: Carmel of Maria Regina, 1961), 34.

to innocent entertainment, for example, while neglecting to work on viewing pornography.

Fasting from your attachments can help loosen their hold on you. Every Lent you practice detachment when you give up things you enjoy. Such fasting jump-starts the detachment process. By the time your fast is over, you have learned to live without the thing you gave up. It is easier to continue to do so going forward. You do not have to permanently give up things that are not sinful, however. Eventually you want to be able to use the material world in an ordered way, in the way God meant you to use it, for his glory.

You can also practice doing everything you do for the motive of pleasing God, rather than any pleasure you receive from your actions. When God's glory comes first in whatever you do, you are truly detached.[54]

See **Questions 97 and 98** for the related subject of mortification.

---

[54] Ibid. 35.

Practicing Meditation

34. *Is Lectio divina the same thing as meditation?*

The Catechism says, "There are as many and varied methods of meditation as there are spiritual masters."[55] Each method of meditation has its singularities, but they all share the goal of pondering the truths of the Faith in order to enter into a closer communion with God. Lectio divina is an ancient method of Christian meditation. Here are the basic steps, as delineated by Guigo II in his twelfth-century book *Ladder of Monks*:

Lectio: slowly and with prayerful attention read a short passage of Scripture, repeatedly if necessary.

Meditatio: ponder what you have read and see how it applies to your life.

Oratio: talk to God about your meditation.

Contemplatio: rest in the Lord as the Scripture sinks deep into your heart.

---

[55] CCC no. 2707.

35. What should I do in the contemplatio step of Lectio divina?

Dan Burke's excellent book *Into the Deep: Finding Peace through Prayer* teaches Lectio divina to beginners. He says about the step of prayer traditionally called *contemplatio*:

> Allow yourself to become absorbed in God's words as he invites you into a deeper kind of prayer, one that will bring you into his presence in ways that purely mental exercises could never achieve. You may not experience this kind of absorption as you initially explore this method of prayer. It can take time to get familiar enough with the process so that it fades into the background and becomes a normal expression of your heart.[56]

The *contemplatio* step is basically the same as the acquired recollection mentioned in **Questions 82, 84, and 108.** If it seems unnatural to you, do not force it. Try to spend a few moments in silent love of God as a response to the earlier steps of prayer. You may have experienced this type of absorption at Adoration. As you advance in prayer, this step will become more natural to you and will begin taking over more of your meditation time.

Other methods of meditation do not include the *contemplatio* as a step, but let it develop organically from your meditation.

---

[56] *Into the Deep: Finding Peace through Prayer* (North Palm Beach: Beacon, 2017), 51.

36. What are some other methods of meditation?

Here is very simple method of meditation:

1. Choose a quiet spot alone to pray.

2. Focus your mind and heart on God.

3. Ask the Holy Spirit to speak to you through the Scriptures.

4. Begin prayerfully reading your chosen passage.

5. When anything moves you, pause. Ponder. Talk to God about what you have read, praise Him, or silently lift your heart to Him in love – whichever you feel moved to do. Make resolutions as they apply to your subject.

6. When your conversation with God dries up, return to your passage.

7. Repeat numbers 5 and 6 until your time is almost ended.

8. End with the Our Father, another vocal prayer of your choice, or a brief word of thanksgiving.

Alternate methods of meditation can be found in *Conversation with Christ* by Peter Thomas Rohrbach, *Time for Prayer* by Fr. Jacques Philippe, and *Introduction to the Devout Life* by Saint Francis de Sales. The exact format is not important, as long as you are pondering the Scriptures, applying them to your life, and conversing with God as a response.

37. What Scriptures should I choose for meditation?

Saints and spiritual theologians recommend the Gospels as being the most appropriate material. Pope Leo XIII wrote:

> By the infinite goodness of God man lived again to the hope of an immortal life, from which he had been cut off, but he cannot attain to it if he strives not to walk in the very footsteps of Christ and conform his mind to Christ's by the meditation of Christ's example. Therefore this is not a counsel but a duty, and it is the duty, not of those only who desire a more perfect life, but clearly of every man "always bearing about in our body the mortification of Jesus."[57]

The purpose of meditation is to get to know and love God better. It's not about studying theology or learning about the lives of the saints. What you read should teach you about God's character and move you to desire a closer relationship with him. Nowhere in the Bible or the writings of the saints do you come face to face with God as powerfully as you do in the Gospels. Jesus reveals the face of God. Every event in his life teaches you who God is and who you are in relationship to him.

When choosing a particular passage from the Gospels, it's best to proceed in an organized fashion, rather than randomly picking a chapter. One good practice is to follow the daily Mass readings, meditating on the Gospel for the day. Another good practice is slowly going through one of the Gospels from beginning to end.

---

[57] *Exuente Iam Anno* no. 10.

Rarely, some people find the Gospels difficult to understand on their own. Others feel drawn to different books of Scripture. The Psalms are particularly moving, and you can find one to suit almost any joy or struggle you may be experiencing. The Psalms offer good material for those who are struggling with dryness in prayer (see **Question 62**). Although they are good for moving the heart, however, they do not always teach you about the character of God at the same level that the Gospels do. For beginners, the Gospels are best.

If you find the Gospels difficult to understand, you might try a book of meditations on Scripture. Fr. Timothy Gallagher provides excellent meditations in *An Ignatian Introduction to Prayer*. Another good aid to meditation on the Gospels is *The Better Part* by Fr. John Bartunek. Some will find the consistent format of the meditations in these books helpful for learning the process of meditating on Scripture. By the time you have finished, you will probably be ready to begin meditating without help.

38. Should I use pre-made meditations or make my own?

Ideally, meditations should come from your heart. However, not everyone has the strong imagination or ability to reflect on Scripture that this requires. The conversation with God is more important than the pondering. As Teresa as Ávila said, "Prayer is not a matter of thinking much, but of loving much. Do whatever leads you to love."[58] If written meditations help you to have a more fruitful prayer time, by all means use them. If you find them unhelpful, don't use them.

---

[58] *Interior Castle* 4, 1.

You should always have at least part of the conversation in your own words, however. Otherwise, you are practicing vocal prayer rather than mental prayer.

39. *What do I do when the Scripture moves me?*

During meditation, if something in the Scripture passage you read moves you, talk to God about it. Thank him, praise him, ask him for grace, et cetera, as appropriate to your meditation. Let it draw you into a more heartfelt conversation with Christ. It is this heart-to-heart exchange, more than any intellectual pondering, that will convert you, helping you to love God better. All earlier steps of mental prayer — entering God's presence, reading Scripture, meditating on it — are means to the end of greater intimacy with Christ. The intimacy blooms in the conversation.

40. *Are the imaginative types of prayer that the Jesuits teach useful?*

Their teaching comes from Saint Ignatius himself. He taught people to imagine themselves in the biblical story they were reading. Some people worry that when using this method they will imagine something unorthodox. When you use the imagination this way in mental prayer, you should stick close to the Scriptures, just as you do with other forms of meditation. You can ask yourself, "If I were present when this event took place, what would I see? What would I hear? What might Jesus say to me personally?" This is simply another way to apply the Scripture to yourself and your situation. It can be very powerful. If this method works for you, moving you toward a meaningful conversation with Christ, feel free to use it.

41. Are there other ways to meditate besides using Scripture?

Some people prefer to use a book of meditations such as *Divine Intimacy* by Fr. Gabriel of Saint Mary Magdalen. Saint Francis de Sales gives a number of sample meditations on biblical themes in *Introduction to the Devout Life*. *The Imitation of Christ* by Thomas à Kempis is also a good source of meditation.

Saint Teresa of Ávila speaks of using sacred art as a starting point for meditation. Another suggestion she makes is to imagine yourself at the side of Christ. For example:

> If you are suffering trials, or sad, look upon Him on His way to the Garden. What sore distress He must have borne in His soul, to describe His own suffering as He did and to complain of it! Or look upon Him bound to the Column, full of pain, His flesh all torn to pieces by His great love for you. How much He suffered, persecuted by some, spat upon by others, denied by His friends, and even deserted by them, with none to take His part, frozen with the cold and left so completely alone that you may well comfort each other! Or look upon Him bending under the weight of the Cross and not even allowed to take breath: He will look upon you with His lovely and compassionate eyes, full of tears, and in comforting your grief will forget His own because you are bear-

ing Him company in order to comfort Him and turning your head to look upon Him.[59]

Generally, these simpler ways of meditation work better for those who have already practiced some meditation on Scripture and are ready for a less analytical stage of meditation (see **Question 83**).

42. *Are resolutions a necessary part of mental prayer?*

Many authorities suggest making a decision to put into practice something specific that comes out of your meditation time. Saint Francis de Sales writes, for example:

> Above all things, my daughter, strive when your meditation is ended to retain the thoughts and resolutions you have made as your earnest practice throughout the day. This is the real fruit of meditation, without which it is apt to be unprofitable, if not actually harmful — inasmuch as to dwell upon virtues without practicing them tends to puff us up with unrealities, until we begin to fancy ourselves all that we have meditated upon and resolved to be; which is all very well if our resolutions are earnest and substantial, but on the contrary hollow and dangerous if they are not put into practice.[60]

If you meditate on humility, for example, and never try to practice it, you are more culpable for any sins of pride than you were before that meditation. You can no longer

---

[59] *Way of Perfection* Chap. 26.
[60] *Introduction to the Devout Life* 2, 8.

claim ignorance. Besides that, you may think yourself advanced in holiness simply because you have thought about humility. Ironically, your meditation on humility has not only failed to inspire you to practice it; it has produced pride in you! This is what Saint Francis calls "unprofitable, if not actually harmful" meditation.

Mental prayer is necessarily linked to conversion. If your prayer is not changing the way you live, something is amiss. Saint Francis wants your resolutions to be "earnest and substantial" so that you follow through on them. New resolutions for each period of mental prayer are not always necessary. Trying to work on too many areas at once usually backfires. However, you should be examining your life in light of the Gospel on a regular basis. A recommitment to a resolution made in the past can also ensure that your conversion is ongoing. But sometimes your mental prayer might be more focused on adoring the Lord, sitting in silent love of him, et cetera, and in these cases specific resolutions would not be necessary.

Listening to God in Prayer

43. *How is silence important for prayer?*

Remember when God spoke to Elijah on Mt. Horeb?

> And he said, "Go forth, and stand upon the mount before the Lord." And behold, the Lord passed by, and a great and strong wind rent the mountains, and broke in pieces the rocks before the Lord, but the Lord was not in the wind; and after the wind an earthquake, but the Lord was not in the earthquake; and after the earthquake a fire, but the Lord was not in the fire; and after the fire a still small voice. And when Elijah heard it, he wrapped his face in his mantle and went out and stood at the entrance of the cave. And behold, there came a voice to him, and said, "What are you doing here, Elijah?"[61]

God desires to commune with us in a "still, small voice." In order to "hear" Him — to be open to receive Him — we must be silent.

---

[61] 1 Kgs 19:11-13.

Saint John of the Cross wrote:

> The Father spoke one Word, which was his Son, and
> this Word he speaks always in eternal silence, and in
> silence must it be heard by the soul.[62]

Silence gives God space in which to speak to you. Prayerful silence goes beyond lack of external noise. Your aim is to rest in God, rather than being restless. When meditating on Scripture, you seek to hear God's voice speaking to you through it, so that you can conform your life to his will. The internal noise of thoughts unrelated to your prayer time can distract you. How often do your thoughts buzz like bees when you sit down to pray, swarming around you, taking your attention off of God?

How can you practice the necessary silence? At prayer time, make a conscious decision to put aside distractions. The first step in prayer is often called "placing yourself in the presence of God" (see **Question 28**). In your heart, move away from your normal occupations. Consciously turn your attention to God instead. You may find praying this verse helpful: "I have stilled and quieted my soul, like a weaned child in its mother's arms."[63] Say it silently or whisper it to God. Then you may find your whirling thoughts settling into silence. Another idea is to picture Jesus on the Cross or in the manger. One by one, lay all your cares at His feet. Leave them there for the duration of your prayer.

Silence might feel uncomfortable at first. That is actually a good sign. You aren't meant to be empty. But you are meant to be filled with God, not temporal things. Empty

---

[62] *Sayings of Light and Love* 100.
[63] Ps 131:2.

your heart of the noise of the world so that you can hear the words God wants to speak to you in his still, small voice.

44. How can I remain quiet to hear the voice of God?

There is a common misconception among people who desire to make their prayer more truly a conversation. They want to be guided by God, to hear his voice. They sit down to pray and they simply listen, waiting for God to speak to their hearts. Sometimes God may speak to you in this way. However, sitting and waiting for God to speak can invite both frustration and deception. If God does not seem to speak, what do you do next? Continue sitting there waiting? Start talking to him? Get up and do something else? On the other hand, if you do encounter some inspirations, insights, or ideas, how can you be sure they come from God? They might just be your own thoughts. They could even be deceptions from the Devil.

The solution to this dilemma is to do something altogether different in prayer. Instead of waiting for God to speak to you directly on any subject at all, you can listen to his voice in Sacred Scripture. The Bible is the Word of God, divinely inspired by the Holy Spirit. When you read it prayerfully, you are reading a message from God. You don't have to ask yourself, "Did God really say that, or was it just my imagination?" You have the text in front of you. You need not go away frustrated, either, wondering why God is silent.

As the Catechism says,

> The Church "forcefully and specially exhorts all the Christian faithful … to learn 'the surpassing

knowledge of Jesus Christ' (*Phil*3:8) by frequent reading of the divine Scriptures.... Let them remember, however, that prayer should accompany the reading of Sacred Scripture, so that a dialogue takes place between God and man. For 'we speak to him when we pray; we listen to him when we read the divine oracles.'"[64]

Practice a good method of meditation like those detailed earlier in this book (**Questions 34-36**). Do not seek an unnatural quieting of the mind that leaves you doing nothing or leads you into deception.

45. How might God speak to me during prayer?

In the early stages of prayer, God primarily speaks to you through the Scriptures and your reflection upon them (see **Question 44**). You must trust the Holy Spirit to guide your prayer and to help you see the areas in which you need to be more converted.

God can also give you a sense of his will about something you were not meditating on. For example, you may have been trying to have a better relationship with a co-worker and not getting very far. Then when you are meditating on the feeding of the 5,000, you suddenly have an idea how you can reach out to that person. It was not directly related to anything you were thinking about at the time. Your idea could well be an inspiration from the Holy Spirit.

Sometimes God speaks to you more directly through specific words, what some might call a word of knowledge or wisdom or encouragement. He can even use locutions or

---

[64] CCC no. 2653, quoting St. Ambrose.

visions. Be careful about putting too much credence in this type of communication without consulting a spiritual director. (See **Question 59.**)

46. How do I know that the voice I am hearing in prayer is really God?

Dan Burke, author and President of the Ávila Institute for Spiritual Formation, has responded to this question recommending that you stay close to the text you are meditating on: "What does the Bible text say in itself? What did the author intend?" He also advises that those who are new to Catholicism or to mental prayer should study the Catechism and the Gospels.[65] These practices minimize the likelihood of deception.

The Discernment of Spirits taught by Saint Ignatius is helpful here as well. Ignatius taught that when you are moving toward God in your spiritual life, consolations in prayer come from him (see **Question 49**). When you are moving away from God, you may experience peaceful or pleasant feelings that in a certain sense mimic consolations. These feelings, however, come from the flesh or the Devil. In both cases, whether consolations or a mimicry of them, they are given to encourage you to *continue* in your chosen direction. Conversely, desolation that comes when you are moving toward God is usually from the flesh or demonic powers (see **Question 50**). Desolation that comes when you are moving

---

[65] From a conversation in my Facebook group Authentic Contemplative Prayer
(https://www.facebook.com/groups/737852419689126/permalink/1384768914997470/). He has a guide on this question in his book *Into the Deep: Finding Peace through Prayer.*

away from God is allowed by God, but not directly given by him. At times the desolation comes through the vehicle of your conscience, for example. Desolation is meant to persuade you to *change* direction.[66]

As you grow in relationship with Christ, it is easier to discern his voice. However, you should always keep in mind that even at stages most of us would consider advanced, deception is still possible. See also **Question 59** on visions and locutions.

47. How can I allow the Holy Spirit to pray through me and for me?

Saint Paul writes,

> Likewise the Spirit helps us in our weakness; for we do not know how to pray as we ought, but the Spirit himself intercedes for us with sighs too deep for words. And he who searches the hearts of men knows what is the mind of the Spirit, because the Spirit intercedes for the saints according to the will of God.[67]

The Holy Spirit guides your prayer in secret. When you have insight into a Scripture verse, when you apply it to your life in a new way, this is the Holy Spirit at work. When you are unable to meditate because of illness or other factors beyond your control, you can trust that the Holy Spirit

---

[66] Whole books have been written on this subject. See, for example, *The Discernment of Spirits* by Fr. Timothy Gallagher. Note also that desolation in prayer is different from the contemplative dryness of the passive nights, which comes from God. See Questions 93-95.

[67] Rom 8:26-27.

is making your prayer efficacious. Sometimes when you are hurting, all you can do is make a silent plea to God for help. This too is "translated" by the Holy Spirit to connect you with God.

However, this passage of Scripture is especially true of contemplation. In contemplation, God infuses a desire for himself that cannot be adequately expressed in words. This longing opens your heart to receive a continually deeper outpouring of God's life and love.

48. What if I am asking for guidance and God is silent?

God gave you a mind so that you would use it to discern his will. In most cases, you just need to ask the Holy Spirit for guidance and then use strategies to reason through what the best decision would be. God more often works in mundane ways than people think. Saint Francis de Sales writes:

> The choice of one's vocation, the planning of some matter of great consequence, of some work occupying much time, of some very great expense, the change of home, the choice of companions, and such things, we should seriously consider what is most according to the will of God. But in little daily matters, in which even a mistake is neither of much consequence nor irreparable, what need is there to make a business of them, to scrutinize them, or to importunely ask advice about them? To what end should I put myself out to learn whether God would prefer me to say the Rosary or Our Lady's Office,

since there can be no such difference between them, that a great examination need be held...[68]

If you have a more serious subject for discernment, such as a vocation, you may want to discuss the issue with a competent spiritual director or priest. Sometimes an objective person can see more clearly how God is leading you than you can yourself.

---

[68] *Treatise on the Love of God* 8, 14.

The Experience of Mental Prayer

49. *What are consolations in prayer?*

Consolation refers to the action or presence of God that you can feel or consciously experience. It moves your heart toward God and causes you to love him more. You might have new insight into the Scriptures, realize how God has been working in your life, feel a sweet peace, or suddenly have the grace to forgive someone who has sinned against you. You might be moved to repentance, have an increase in faith, hope, or love, or simply feel a deep desire to give everything to the Lord.[69]

God gives you consolations so that you will learn to love him above all things. Consolations give you the strength to give up the things you know are outside God's will for you. It is especially common for people who are just beginning a life of prayer to experience consolations. God is rewarding their efforts and encouraging them to continue.

---

[69] See "Spiritual Dictionary," *SpiritualDirection.com*, https://spiritualdirection.com/2013/11/07/consolation-navigating-the-interior-life-spiritual-dictionary. Accessed 5/30/19.

However, the flesh and the Devil can give a false sense of peace and security that mimics consolation to those who are moving away from God (see **Question 52**).

50. *What is desolation?*

Desolation is the opposite of consolation (see **Question 49**). Saint Ignatius of Loyola taught:

> I call desolation all the contrary of [consolation], such as darkness of soul, disturbance in it, movement to low and earthly things, disquiet from various agitations and temptations, moving to lack of confidence, without hope, without love, finding oneself totally slothful, tepid, sad, and, as if separated from one's Creator and Lord.[70]

Desolation comes from the flesh or the Devil. God allows desolation, using it to bring you to repentance and renewed fervor when you have been moving away from him. You might feel a prick of the conscience when you do something you know is against God's will. Then later, if you have not repented, you might feel restless and distant from God. You need to change direction, reorienting yourself toward God, and the desolation moves you to do so. It can be a powerful and dark desolation in a person in a state of mortal sin, requiring a complete turnaround, or a lighter sense of guilt in someone who had been following God, but purposely chose an evil act, requiring an acknowledgment of sin and a renewed resolution of obedience.

---

[70] *The Spiritual Exercises,* Fourth Rule, quoted by Fr. Timothy M. Gallagher, OMV, in *The Discernment of Spirits: An Ignatian Guide for Everyday Living* (Chestnut Ridge, NY: Crossroads, 2005), 60.

Desolation from the flesh is often rooted in something as simple as ill health or lack of sleep. This physical weakness can morph into a spiritual malaise. The Devil gives desolation in order to draw a person away from following God. He makes the person feel that following God is not worth the personal sacrifice. See **Questions 51 and 52** for more on consolation and desolation.

51. Should prayer normally be consoling and peaceful?

You may be relieved (or frightened) to discover that the answer is *no!* Saint Ignatius teaches that prayer alternates between consolation and desolation, between sweetness and difficulty, the felt action or presence of God and the seeming absence of God.[71] Yet most people have the idea that something is wrong if they are not experiencing consolation. In a sense there is something wrong, but it is man's fallen state or the battle against demonic forces, which will always affect you in this life. As long as you are on this side of heaven, there will be desolation, dryness, and distractions. These result from physical, mental, and spiritual weakness, and sometimes the direct action of God to draw you closer to himself.

Saint Ignatius says that just as Joseph in the Old Testament stored up food in the seven years of plenty, knowing that seven years of famine were coming, so you should use the time of consolation to prepare yourself for the desolation that will follow.[72] When you are in desolation, you

---

[71] I recommend *The Discernment of Spirits* for an in-depth explication of St. Ignatius' teaching.
[72] *Discernment of Spirits* 133.

should also keep in mind that it is a temporary state and that consolation will eventually return.[73]

Enjoy the consolation God gives you. Thank him for it, and use it to grow in divine intimacy. But remember that consolation is not necessarily a sign of holiness, nor is desolation necessarily a sign of God's disfavor. Both experiences are necessary for spiritual growth.

52. How do I know if my consolations come from God?

Saint Ignatius said that the first step in determining the source of your consolations is determining whether you are moving toward or away from God.

When a person is moving away from God, or is comfortable in his sin, the Devil and the flesh (Saint Ignatius includes them both in his term "the enemy") do not want him to change. The enemy may produce pleasant feelings in this person's soul so that he remains content in doing evil. He might entice him with thoughts of material pleasure, false freedom, or power. These are not properly called *consolation,* because they tempt him to keep his back turned to God. However, the person experiencing them — especially experiencing feelings of peace and contentment — easily takes them as a sign that all is well in his life.

On the other hand, when the person is moving toward God, trying to make changes to come closer to him, the enemy will try to make him desolate so that he abandons the path of prayer and virtue.[74] Feelings of peace and contentment are more likely true consolations from God for such a

---

[73] Ibid. 107.
[74] *Discernment of Spirits* 31-33.

person. Therefore, a person who is open to God and moving toward him can generally assume that any positive experiences in prayer are consolations from God. God is encouraging the soul to keep moving forward.[75]

When you receive consolations, you should quickly turn from them to God himself. Remaining fixed on the consolations can cause you to become attached to them and begin seeking them instead of seeking God. The very best test of the origin of these experiences is whether they cause you to continue moving forward, with even more zeal, or they cause you to fall back or become complacent.

53. Should I empty myself in prayer?

In Christian prayer, you never try to empty the mind of all thoughts through human efforts. You use the mind to focus on God and the heart to love him. There is a type of emptying of oneself that the saints speak of, however. The Congregation for the Doctrine of the Faith (CDF) says,

> The emptiness which God requires is that of the renunciation of personal selfishness, not necessarily that of the renunciation of those created things which he has given us and among which he has placed us.[76]

You should not reject God's gift of the intellect, will, imagination, and memory. Instead, you order them (and everything else) toward God's will. You empty yourself of selfish clinging to material objects and of deliberate sin. Sur-

---

[75] Of course, extraordinary phenomena, such as visions and locutions, require special cautions. See Question 59.
[76] *On Some Aspects of Christian Meditation* no. 19.

rendering your will to God includes growing at the pace he sets, instead of trying to run ahead. Some people mistakenly think that if they just sit quietly in prayer, without trying to think or feel anything, God will come to them in an intimate way. But they have neglected to prepare for his coming. This preparation involves faithfulness to daily meditation on Scripture, and living a virtuous life. It is a life of continual conversion.

When God begins giving you the gift of infused contemplation, he will make meditation difficult, if not impossible. At that time, your prayer should change. You must do your best *then* to sit quietly in his presence and embrace the hidden working of the Holy Spirit. This is the beginning of what Saint John of the Cross calls the passive night of the senses (see **Questions 93-96**). Before you assume that you are at this stage and try to remain "passive" in prayer, however, you should consult a spiritual director or knowledgeable and orthodox priest. Most people who think they are in the passive night are mistaken. Becoming passive too soon can harm your spiritual life.

See the section **Meditation: Christian Versus Non-Christian** for more on erroneous ideas about prayer.

54. Is it okay to listen to music while I pray?

Many beginners in mental prayer do use sacred music as a background to their prayer. However, most eventually abandon the practice, opting for silence. If it helps you to establish a habit of mental prayer, you may use it for that purpose, but once you've established the habit, let go of the music. It is too easy to be moved by the melody rather than by the goodness of God. Music with lyrics could cause you to focus on things that God is not leading you to focus on at particular times. The music could also become a source of attachment, so that you are unable to pray well without it. You must slowly give up your dependence on anything but God if you want to continue growing. You cannot enter fully into the passive night of the senses (see **Question 93**) while holding onto sensible delight in music.

Saint John of the Cross writes:

> I should like to offer a norm for discerning when this gratification of the senses is beneficial and when not. Whenever spiritual persons, on hearing music or other things, seeing agreeable objects, smelling sweet fragrance, or feeling the delight of certain tastes and delicate touches, immediately, at the first movement direct their thought and the affection of their will to God, receiving more satisfaction in the thought of God than in the sensible object that caused it, and find no delight in the senses save for this motive, it is a sign that they are profiting by the senses and the sensory part is a help to the spirit…. Yet anyone who does not feel this freedom of spirit in these objects and sensible delights, but finds that the will pauses in and feeds on them, suffers harm from them and ought to turn from their use.[77]

If you tend to delight in listening to music (and not necessarily sacred music), humming catchy tunes and playing music for enjoyment outside of prayer, you are possibly attached to music. John teaches that all things that come to

---

[77] *The Ascent of Mt. Carmel* 3, 24.

you through your senses should lead you to God. As long as you enjoy thinking about music more than you enjoy thinking about God, or as long as you enjoy listening to music more than you do spending time with God in prayer, you show that you are attached to it. You are making music an end in itself rather than letting it lead you to God. John would have you fast from listening to music *at all* until you are more detached, let alone during your prayer time.

Of course, detachment is gradual, but it is necessary. Besides, isn't our culture already being drowned in man-made noise? Form the habit of praying in silence and the silence will become a treasure to you. And you will also learn to love music for the Lord's sake, as John himself did.

See **Questions 31-33** for more on detachment.

55. Is it okay to spend my mental prayer time talking to God about my difficulties?

Normally you should spend your mental prayer time pondering Scripture and entering into dialog with God based on what you have read. Petitions are best offered in your vocal prayer time, such as a daily Rosary. This practice keeps mental prayer focused on deepening your relationship with Jesus, rather than on having your needs met. Imagine if every time you got together with a friend, he spent most of the time asking you for favors. Would that relationship be likely to grow deeper?

God is, of course, concerned for even your smallest needs. The Scripture says that "your Father knows your need before you ask him,"[78] but sometimes all you may be able to do in prayer is express the heaviness in your heart. If

---

[78] Mt 6:8.

you can, place your needs before him briefly, then return to your regular practice of meditating on Scripture. Leaving your needs in God's hands will increase your trust, which is a necessary foundation for deepening prayer.

56. Can mental prayer be a communal activity?

Some religious orders have practiced mental prayer at the same time, each person in his or her choir stall, for centuries. Some secular order members pray mental prayer in common at monthly gatherings. Also, many people do mental prayer at Eucharistic Adoration, when others are present, or belong to a communal Lectio divina group (see **Question 34**).

There cannot, then, be a strict negative answer to this question. However, for lay people of today, communal prayer can sometimes hinder growth. Like many other practices, it may be useful to beginners who have not yet formed a habit of prayer. But for those not obliged to pray with others, communal mental prayer can hinder the individual freedom that is a prerequisite for full surrender to God. Each person grows at his own pace; the Holy Spirit acts in each heart uniquely. Communal meditations may be too advanced for some, too basic for others. There is also the danger that lay people will reserve their mental prayer to common prayer times and neglect spending time with God alone. Since lay people do not generally live in community, that could mean praying mental prayer only once a week or less. They might feel uncomfortable praying in solitude, if they have been always used to praying with others. Yet, the saints have always insisted on solitude — at the very least, mental solitude — as a necessary component of mental prayer.

Make use of communal mental prayer if it helps you, but be ready to leave it behind when the Holy Spirit moves you to do so. And make sure you are praying daily in silence and solitude between these communal times.

57. Can mental prayer be addressed to a saint or the Blessed Virgin Mary?

You can pray to Mary or one of the other saints as a part of mental prayer. However, the purpose of mental prayer is to grow in intimacy with Christ. This intimacy comes about through spending time alone with him. Therefore, the bulk of mental prayer time should be directed toward God himself. If you pray from the heart to Mary and the saints, you should not cut short your time with God to do so. Saint Francis de Sales mentions addressing the angels and saints in mental prayer "occasionally," especially when you have meditated on a Scripture passage that speaks of a particular saint.[79] You can use vocal prayer, such as the Rosary or litanies, as a separate practice for regularly invoking the saints.

58. Should prayer before the Blessed Sacrament be different than prayer at home?

There is no reason it needs to be. If you meditate on Scripture for mental prayer, that is an excellent practice to follow in Adoration. However, many people do find it easier to enter the prayer of simple gaze (or acquired recollection; see **Question 84**) when before the Blessed Sacrament. For short periods, they find no text or image is needed, as they

---

[79] *Introduction to the Devout Life* 2, 8.

are gazing at the Body of the Lord. You should not force yourself to sit silently in this way, whether at home or in the Adoration chapel. But in either case, if you feel moved to a silent gaze of love, you should follow that impulse. The difference is that in mental prayer at home it is generally advisable to start with reading Scripture so that your prayer does not become self-indulgent by focusing on your needs and desires instead of letting God take the lead. Without a text to meditate on, you are also more likely to suffer from distractions.

59. What if I experience visions or locutions during prayer?

Visions and locutions fall under what are called *extraordinary phenomena* (see **Question 103**). That means they are not necessary for sanctity, nor are they a sign that you are close to God. Some saints had few, if any, of these experiences. Others experienced them repeatedly. If you are still in the purgative way (see **Question 83**), it is less likely that you will experience extraordinary phenomena during mental prayer.[80]

More often, you may sense at times that God is impressing something on your heart. These impressions may then be translated by you into words, often in a stumbling manner that is significantly different than the precise clarity of locutions.

---

[80] See John of the Cross, *The Ascent of Mt. Carmel* 2, 29. Readers in the Charismatic movement may experience these phenomena at prayer meetings, et cetera. But they should at least begin their mental prayer time meditating on Scripture, just like everyone else, and not look for visions or other extraordinary phenomena.

Teresa of Ávila writes:

> The first and truest [sign of authentic locutions] is the sense of power and authority which they bear with them, both in themselves and in the actions which follow them. I will explain myself further. A soul is experiencing all the interior disturbances and tribulations which have been described, and all the aridity and darkness of the understanding. A single word of this kind — just a "Be not troubled" — is sufficient to calm it. No other word need be spoken; a great light comes to it; and all its trouble is lifted from it, although it had been thinking that, if the whole world, and all the learned men in the world, were to combine to give it reasons for not being troubled, they could not relieve it from its distress, however hard they might strive to do so....

> The second sign is that a great tranquility dwells in the soul, which becomes peacefully and devoutly recollected, and ready to sing praises to God....

> The third sign is that these words do not vanish from the memory for a very long time: some, indeed, never vanish at all.[81]

People are often mistaken about the source of their visions and locutions. Just think about how many "apparitions" the Church has deemed unworthy of belief. It is more likely that your own psyche is calling up words or pictures than that God is communicating with you in this way. God's

---

[81] *Interior Castle* 4, 3.

usual way of communicating with those in the purgative way during prayer is through the Scriptures.[82] The Devil can also give false visions and locutions, so you should not automatically assume that they are revelations from God. In fact, taking them with some amount of skepticism is usually more profitable.

John of the Cross gives surprising advice about extraordinary phenomena. He says not even to analyze them to figure out whether they are from the Lord or not. John wants you to be preoccupied with nothing but God, and these phenomena tend to draw attention to themselves. They can make you proud, lead you astray, or make you attached to experiences of God, rather than to God himself. John counsels you to tell your spiritual director about such phenomena and then go on as if they had never happened. If they were really from God, he says, they accomplished God's work in you at the moment he gave them.[83] If they are meant to be shared with anyone else, that is up to your spiritual director. Don't tell anyone else about them unless your director instructs you to do so. Put them out of your memory as much as you can and return to praying as usual.

60. Is there a connection between dreams and mental prayer?

While God can speak to you through your dreams, it is generally unprofitable to spend too much time analyzing them in order to find divine meaning in them. If God wants to speak to you through your dreams, he will make it very

---

[82] Of course, for those in the illuminative way or beyond, God communicates his very self, beyond words or images.
[83] *The Ascent of Mt. Carmel* 2, 11.

clear that he is doing so and laborious dream-analysis will not be necessary. Dream interpretation is usually associated with Jungian psychology, which is connected to the New Age movement. Therefore, those who focus on interpreting dreams often have other New Age practices or beliefs. Focusing on your dreams as a possible source of communication from God is just the sort of focusing on extraordinary phenomena that Saint John of the Cross warned against (see **Question 59**).

61. What if God does not answer my prayers?

It's always difficult when prayers seem to go unanswered. Some people will automatically assume that your faith is deficient if God is not answering you. But prayer is not about persuading God to conform to your will. It's about learning to conform to God's will. You must be ready to receive in prayer whatever God deems best for you on a given day. Some days that will be just what you thought you needed. Other days it may seem the opposite of what you needed.

Ultimately, only God himself can say for certain why he is not answering your prayers, but here are some possibilities:

- You are asking for something that would not be good for you.
- You are asking for something that he will eventually give you, but it's the wrong time.
- He is answering your prayer in a way you did not expect and perhaps don't recognize.
- He wants you to learn perseverance in prayer.

- He wants you to learn to trust him.
- You are not making the changes in your life that would enable you to accept his gifts.

Try to keep your prayer focused on meditation, rather than on your needs. As your prayer deepens, you may have a different idea of what you really need and want in life and you will begin to appreciate the times that God says *no* to your requests.

Difficulties in Meditation

62. Why is it sometimes so hard to meditate?

Difficulty or dryness (lack of consolation; see **Question 49**) in prayer is perfectly normal. It could have a variety of causes. Sometimes prayer is dry because you are sick, depressed, anxious, or over-tired. In such cases, dryness is usually temporary. A little bit of reflection can pinpoint the reason for the dryness. When you catch up on your sleep, recover your health, or solve the problems that are causing anxiety, the dryness disappears.

Other times, dryness is caused by unconfessed sin or a lack of trust in God. The solution in these cases is repentance and deeper conversion.

Sometimes, dryness comes from the Devil's efforts to persuade you to give up prayer (see **Question 50** on desolation).

Still other times, God may be weaning you from dependence on consolations during prayer. As a good Parent, he is helping you grow up. God does this periodically in the early years of the spiritual life. As you mature, you should reach a stage in which the dryness becomes more constant, to the point that you can hardly meditate any more. This is the beginning of the transition to contemplation. In such dryness, you need to surrender to the secret working of the Holy Spirit, rather than trying to force yourself to continue meditating. See **Questions 93-95 and 110** for more on the transition to contemplation and how to behave while experiencing it.

If you experience prolonged dryness in prayer for which there is no obvious cause, consult a spiritual director or knowledgeable and devout priest for help. The different causes of dryness call for different responses and it is imperative to respond appropriately if you wish to continue to grow. Saint Francis de Sales includes an entire chapter on dryness (Part 4, chapter 14) in *Introduction to the Devout Life.*

63. What should I do when I cannot recollect myself for prayer?

When your mind just won't seem to focus, remind yourself that the Holy Spirit is still at work in your prayer.[84] Prayer does not depend so much on the success of your efforts as on God's work deep within your soul when you surrender to him.

Never cut your prayer time short because it is difficult. Perseverance is necessary for continued growth. Here are some things you might try:

- Slowly say the Our Father or another vocal prayer.
- Focus on a simple mental image, such as the Eucharist or the flames of the Holy Spirit.

[84] See Rom 8:26.

- Pray a psalm that corresponds to what is happening in your life.
- Repeat a Bible verse that you have found moving in the past.
- Be content to simply receive the Lord's love rather than striving to offer what you do not have to give.

64. If I seem to get nothing out of my meditation, how should I spend my time?

If you try to meditate on Scripture and no insights come to you, do the best you can to remain in God's presence. You might try a different passage of Scripture or one of the other suggestions from **Question 63**. If you feel moved to talk to God heart-to-heart, go ahead and do so. If you feel drawn to sitting in silent love of him, that is even better.

Don't worry yourself with trying twenty different solutions in one prayer time. Making a reasonable effort is enough. Once again, however, make sure not to cut your time short simply because it is difficult. Prayer is more efficacious when it is difficult than when it is easy.

65. What if I'm too drowsy when I pray?

Saint Thérèse of Lisieux famously used to fall asleep during mental prayer. She writes:

> I remember that little children are as pleasing to their parents when they are asleep as well as when they are wide awake; I remember, too, that when they perform operations, doctors put their patients

to sleep. Finally, I remember that: "The Lord knows our weakness, that he is mindful that we are but dust and ashes."[85]

Saint Thérèse's words, of course, only apply if you are not negligent. Do your best to go to bed at a reasonable time and get enough sleep. Pray at your best time of the day. If necessary, try changing your position to kneeling or standing. Experiment with praying aloud or do more reading and less analyzing of the text. Sometimes physiologically you just can't help your drowsiness. God can work through your bodily weaknesses. Just do the best you can and don't worry about it.

66. Is it okay to drink coffee when I pray?

Coffee or tea right before prayer — or even during prayer in absolute necessity — can help the person with fatigue to stay awake and alert. Generally speaking, you would not want to consume anything during mental prayer, because it takes your attention off of God when you pause to drink. But if it is truly the only way you can keep yourself from falling asleep, you can do this sparingly. Then after you finish praying, think about how you can change your routine or lifestyle so you don't become dependent on caffeine for attentive prayer.

---

[85] St. Thérèse of Lisieux, *Story of a Soul: The Autobiography of St. Thérèse of Lisieux* (Washington, DC: ICS, 1996), 199.

67. How can I pray with brain fog caused by illness?

First, be consoled with the realization that you are not alone. Many people with chronic illnesses struggle with this problem. Some of them enjoy a deep prayer life. No physical, mental, or emotional defect (unless it is the result of ongoing sin) can keep you from intimacy with Christ, provided you surrender to him and persevere.[86] Follow the advice in **Questions 65 and 66** regarding drowsiness. If you can, speak to a spiritual director to get more specific help with your situation.

68. How can I overcome distractions?

Distractions in prayer are perfectly normal. Everyone encounters them. After revealing that she suffered from terrible distractions for years, Saint Teresa writes:

> Just as we cannot stop the movement of the heavens, revolving as they do with such speed, so we cannot restrain our thought. And then we send all the faculties of the soul after it, thinking we are lost, and have misused the time that we are spending in the presence of God. Yet the soul may perhaps be wholly united with Him in the Mansions very near His presence, while thought remains in the outskirts of the castle, suffering the assaults of a thousand wild and venomous creatures and from this suffering winning merit. So this must not upset us, and we

---

[86] See Rom 8:35-39.

must not abandon the struggle, as the devil tries to make us do. Most of these trials and times of unrest come from the fact that we do not understand ourselves.[87]

One of the biggest mistakes people make about distractions is worrying too much over them. Some people are so concerned about their wandering minds that they drive themselves to distraction, if you'll forgive the pun, seeking a solution. Some look for a secret to overcoming them. They might turn to techniques like mindfulness (see **Question 73**), then spend more time practicing hyper-focusing than they do talking to God.

That is not the route you want to go, but neither should you lazily let your mind wander. Let's consider a few alternatives to both extremes. One of the easiest ways to minimize distractions is to pray first thing in the morning. If that is not possible, try some quiet activity before prayer, such as a little reading or a crossword puzzle, as a calming transition. Coloring books for adults are a current fad. Adults should not use one during prayer, no matter how religious its themes, but coloring books could be helpful as a transition to prayer. Using digital media just before prayer almost always causes distractions. That also goes for listening to music. Practice moderation in your media usage and you will be able to focus on God more easily. Other important practices are getting enough sleep and avoiding praying just after a protein-rich meal.

The format of your prayer can help you keep your mind on God. You might start by picturing yourself laying dis-

---

[87] *Interior Castle* 4, 1.

tractions at Jesus' feet. Or ask your guardian angel to keep distractions at bay. If a certain person comes to mind during prayer, briefly pray for him or her if appropriate, then turn your thoughts back to God. Sometimes (though rarely) such thoughts can be from the Holy Spirit, but you don't want to follow rabbit trails. Be discerning.

Your distractions might indicate virtues you need to cultivate or disordered attachments. Turn gently back to God as well as you can while you are praying. After you finish prayer, reflect for a few moments on what distracted you. If you kept rehearsing an argument, for example, ask yourself why it's so important to you. Do you always need to be right? Are you overly critical? Do you care too much about trivial things? Getting to the root of your distractions helps more than just trying to ignore them does.

Distractions cannot harm your prayer unless you consent to them. Used prudently, they may even bring you closer to your goal, which is intimacy with Christ.

69. How can I overcome lustful and blasphemous thoughts in prayer?

This problem is surprisingly common and has even affected John of the Cross and other saints. The Devil often tempts people with evil thoughts during prayer in order to persuade them to give up prayer. Some people also experience an increase in evil thoughts when going through passive purgation (that is, the passive dark nights; see **Question 93**). John writes:

> God generally sends these storms and trials in this
> sensory night and purgation to those he will

afterward put in the other night [of the spirit] — although not all pass on to it — so that thus chastised and buffeted, the senses and faculties may gradually be exercised, prepared, and inured for the union with wisdom that will be granted there. For if a soul is not tempted, tried, and proved through temptations and trials, its senses will not be strengthened in preparation for wisdom.... By these trials it is truly humbled in preparation for its coming exaltation.[88]

So how do you deal with these temptations? As with many things in the spiritual life, the remedy depends on the cause of the thoughts and on your spiritual stage. When temptation to evil thoughts comes from the flesh or the world, a change of lifestyle should help. Avoid bad company. Give up watching movies or reading books with explicit sexuality, significant bad language, or irreverence toward God and others. When the bad thoughts hit you, turn your mind to something else.

Unlike when dealing with other temptations, saints and spiritual writers advise that temptations to lust and blasphemy should not be met head-on. Instead of trying to fight them or practice the opposite virtue, meditate on Christ, especially the Passion.[89] Filling your mind with good thoughts tends to drive away evil thoughts.

If you are in the passive night of the senses, meditation will be difficult to impossible. In that case, try to ignore these and any other irrelevant thoughts that would intrude

---

88 *The Dark Night of the Soul* 1, 14.
89 *Introduction to the Devout Life* 3, 13.

on your time alone with God and take away your peace and surrender to him. Console yourself with the quote from John, above. These trials are usually temporary, and God allows them in order to strengthen you. They can be a sign that he is calling you to deep communion with him.

If you suffer from scrupulosity (which is also common in the passive night of the senses) or from Obsessive-Compulsive Disorder, speak to your spiritual director or a good priest and follow the directions he gives you. Evil thoughts can be especially trying for such people.

Do not let lustful and blasphemous thoughts make you anxious, or the problem will only worsen. Above all, do not give up prayer. If you patiently and humbly persevere, this trial will one day pass.

70. Why does it seem nothing happens in my prayer until the last five minutes?

Our Lord answered this question when speaking to Saint Faustina Kowalska:

> My daughter, in your heart I find everything that so great a number of souls refuses Me. Your heart is My repose. I often wait with great graces until toward the end of prayer.[90]

---

[90] *Divine Mercy in My Soul: Diary of Sister M. Faustina Kowalska* (Stockbridge: Marians of the Immaculate Conception, 1996), no. 268

Now, for those who are somewhat less holy than Saint Faustina was, God may have other reasons for delaying His obvious intervention until the end of prayer. Among them may be:

- He is calling you to persevere.

- He does not want you to judge the quality of your prayer time by your felt experiences.

- What you see as "nothing" may actually be God working in secret.

- You are taking a long time to fully set aside distractions and give your heart to God.

- He is preparing you for a time of drier, purgative prayer (see **Question 93**).

Meditation: Christian Versus Non-Christian

71. How is Christian meditation different from eastern (non-Christian) meditation?

Here are some basic differences between the two:

- Eastern meditation has the goal of losing one's sense of a separate self.[91] Christian meditation has the goal of union of the self with the Triune God through Jesus. You maintain your sense of identity. This union with God constitutes human happiness.

- Eastern meditation is a matter of technique. Christian meditation is a matter of love.

- In eastern meditation, the practitioner sets aside all thoughts. In Christian meditation, the practitioner uses thoughts to draw close to God.

---

[91] For Buddhists, this loss of a separate sense of self helps to eliminate suffering. For Hindus, everyone and everything is a manifestation of the one "Ultimate Reality."

- Eastern meditation seeks to change one's consciousness. Christian meditation seeks to change one's heart and moral life.

Any practice that focuses heavily on technique (or method), fails to address God, and sets aside all thoughts is not Christian prayer. Centering Prayer is one popular practice that is essentially the same as eastern meditation techniques, although there are slight differences in the methods used.[92]

72. Is eastern meditation a help or a hindrance?

The prior of the Grande Chartreuse monastery in France, Fr. Dysmus de Lassus, says:

> The heart of the Christian faith is the Revelation, already in the Old Testament, but more totally by Jesus, of a personal God (tri personal, we might say) who created us to enter into a relationship of love with us....

> My experience of 24 years as master of novices is that those who have touched to [that is, experienced] the Oriental meditation become incapable, despite the years, to grasp the heart of the Christian mystery, there is always an aspect of fusion in the great all that remains, this seems irrepressible.[93]

---

[92] For more information on the problems with Centering Prayer, see Questions 76-80 and my book *Is Centering Prayer Catholic?*
[93] "Syncretism," *Quies*,
http://www.quies.org/quies_syncretism.php.
Accessed. 5/25/19. Spelling and punctuation as in the original translation from French.

In other words, once you have practiced eastern meditation techniques, it's almost impossible for you to shake the belief that you are meant to lose your personality and become one with the universe or "the great all."[94] Instead of prayer being a communion with the Triune God through Jesus Christ, it remains an impersonal technique. You lose the sense that prayer is Love seeking love, that, in the words of the Congregation for the Doctrine of the Faith, "The essential element of authentic Christian prayer is the meeting of two freedoms, the infinite freedom of God with the finite freedom of man."[95] A serious detriment to your faith may result: neglecting the need for salvation through Jesus and relying on human action instead.

Eastern meditation inoculates a person against the Faith. A little bit of "spiritual, but not religious" practice seems to fill the need for the transcendent so that one no longer seeks God. Eastern meditation, at least as practiced by those in the West who are not themselves Buddhists or Hindus, requires no conversion of heart in order to "work." Results are built into the techniques themselves. If you already feel at peace, in harmony with the universe, why turn to a God who requires a radical change of life? Dabbling in these non-Christian practices is not neutral. It is dangerous to the soul.[96]

---

[94] Fr. de Lassus does not distinguish between the goals of Buddhist and Hindu forms of meditation in this passage.

[95] *On Some Aspects of Christian Meditation* no. 3.

[96] I am speaking of Christians taking up these practices. People who have grown up in eastern religions may be doing the best they know how when they meditate. For a Christian to do so is to implicitly reject the Catholic Faith.

73. *Is mindfulness compatible with mental prayer?*

In this answer, *mindfulness* refers to a specific practice that is commonly recommended by self-help and health professionals in both secular and Christian circles. It does not mean the same thing as being mindful of or thinking about God.

Practitioners and defenders of mindfulness almost always say, "Mindfulness is just being aware of the present moment." What could be harmful about that? In fact, they rightly point out that the saints tell us to live in the present, for that is the only place we can find God and his grace. However, the current mindfulness fad is not just a neutral way of being present, it is a Buddhist way.

Almost all mindfulness programs, including the MBSR[97] and "Catholic Mindfulness," instruct you to practice a body scan, breath awareness, or a similar technique for two twenty-minute periods a day. Although the instructor(s) may not tell you so, these techniques come directly from Buddhism. In fact, they are the meditation techniques that Buddhists practice regularly. Most mindfulness practitioners, if you ask them a few questions, admit that they are doing these exercises to undergird their mindfulness.

Mindfulness is the vehicle Buddhists use to acquire a realization that there is no unique, permanent soul, that one's sense of self is an illusion that causes suffering. Since the Buddhist worldview and Buddhist goals are opposed to Christian ones, Buddhist practices are not helpful to attain

---

[97] Mindfulness-Based Stress Reduction, the program created by Jon Kabat-Zinn, which popularized using mindfulness for psychological and physical health.

Christian ends. In fact, they are a hindrance. If you lose the sense of yourself as a person, how can you have a relationship with God? Yet that loss of a sense of self is what mindfulness was created for. Centuries of Buddhist practice show that it works. (See **Question 72** for more on eastern meditation in general.)

Some have suggested that mindfulness is essentially the same as practicing the presence of God, which was most famously taught by Carmelite Brother Lawrence of the Resurrection. This is false, though there is a similarity in how the practices fit into the religions they arise from. Mindfulness is to Buddhist meditation as practicing the presence of God is to prayer. Mindfulness flows out of and leads back to deeper Buddhist meditation, moving one toward nirvana.[98] Practicing the presence of God flows out of and leads back to deeper mental prayer, moving one toward union with God. Mindfulness is connected to Buddhist detachment, which sees all things, even the self, as transitory and ultimately unreal. Practicing the presence of God is connected to Christian detachment, which is founded on a love for God that makes everything else pale. Trying to practice Christian detachment by pure technique is an implicit attempt to circumvent conversion. It takes one toward a non-Christian view of the spiritual life. Techniques alone cannot bring you closer to God, because union with God involves the will — that is, conforming your will to God's. Union is a matter of love.

Besides that, no saint practiced the presence of God in order to calm his thoughts or attain psychological peace.

---

[98] Nirvana, meaning *extinguished* (as in a flame that is blown out), is the goal of Buddhism, in which one's separate-self sense disappears, extinguishing desire and suffering.

The presence of God is not a means to an end. It is itself the end toward which all things should lead us — communing with God always and everywhere, in every activity. In practicing the presence of God, we continually turn to God, rather than turning toward the world of the senses or away from thoughts and feelings.

Another problematic aspect of mindfulness is that the awareness it cultivates is non-judgmental of all thoughts and feelings. Christians *should* judge some of their thoughts as coming from God or from the enemy. This judgment forms the basis of the Discernment of Spirits taught by Saint Ignatius (see **Questions 49-52**). You should not treat all thoughts or feelings as the same. Some you must act on. Others you must reject. Some may be inspirations from the Holy Spirit that you are meant to ponder.

Neither is it necessary for Christians to focus on sensory things in order to live in the present. You can move right to thinking about God and his will for you without this intermediate step. At every moment, have the disposition of openness to God's will. What is the Holy Spirit asking of you now? How can you obey with your whole heart? How should you love God or neighbor in this moment? This open disposition is what the saints mean by living in the present. It has nothing to do with noticing colors, shapes, and textures, but everything to do with finding the hidden God in the duties of your state in life.

If you want to increase your awareness of God's presence, practice daily mental prayer, not Buddhist meditation techniques.

For an excellently researched explanation of mindfulness and the problems it entails for Christians, see *The Catholic Guide to Mindfulness* by Susan Brinkmann.

74. Is it okay to use mantras in prayer?

According to the Oxford English Dictionary, a *mantra* is "a word or a sound repeated to aid concentration in meditation." Mantras originated as words or phrases in Hinduism. They were thought to bring mystical enlightenment, provided the words were pronounced correctly. [99]

Christian prayer does not use mantras. It uses words as a means of communication with God, not as an aid to concentration. Even in repetitive vocal prayers (such as the Rosary), the emphasis for Christians is never on the *sound* of the words, but on their *meaning*.

When the New Age Movement started in the 1970s, some Christians took up mantras. In a document on the New Age written by the Pontifical Councils for Culture and Interreligious Dialogue, we read,

> The point of New Age techniques is to reproduce mystical states[100] at will, as if it were a matter of laboratory material ... hypnosis, mantras, fasting, sleep deprivation and transcendental meditation are attempts to control these states and to experience them continuously.[101]

---

[99] "Mantra," *New World Encyclopedia*, http://www.newworldencyclopedia.org/entry/Mantra. Accessed 5/31/19.

[100] *Mystical* means *secret or hidden*. *Mysticism* in the Catholic conception is generally synonymous with contemplation, although it can also refer to receiving private revelations or other extraordinary phenomena. *Mystical states* in this passage refers to the experience of contemplation, reproduced through altered states of consciousness.

[101] *Jesus Christ, Bearer of the Water of Life: a Christian Reflection on the "New Age"* no. 4, quoting author Michel Lacroix,

Mantras seek to manipulate the human mind or God or gods in order to produce a particular state of consciousness, similar to the experience of hypnotism or psychotropic drugs. Christian prayer, in contrast, is not a matter of control. It is a matter of surrender. A Christian cannot enter a mystical state "at will." Mystical states, if they are truly Christian, are produced by God. In fact, a *mystical state* in Christianity means a stage of the spiritual life in which one experiences union with God through contemplation.

In recent decades, some Catholics have taught a mantra-method of prayer that is a slight adaptation of (Hindu) Transcendental Meditation. Fr. John Main and Fr. Laurence Freeman are the leaders of this mantra movement. (Fr. Main is now deceased.) They falsely interpret the writings of the Desert Fathers and the anonymous fourteenth-century book *The Cloud of Unknowing* to support their teaching. [102]

Christian prayer is about an exchange of love between God and the soul (or at least a conversation on a basic level), not altered states reached through repeated words, sounds, or movements, or focusing on one's breath.

---

http://www.vatican.va/roman_curia/pontifical_councils/interelg/d ocuments/rc_pc_interelg_doc_20030203_new-age_en.html#fn70. Accessed 5/31/19.

[102] For more details on the teaching of Frs. Main and Freeman and the problems associated with it, see David Torkington's article, "Genuine Christian Meditation and Its Counterfeit," at *Spiritual Direction.com,* https://spiritualdirection.com/2018/09/20/genuine-christian-meditation-and-its-counterfeit-part-13-mini-course-on-prayer.

75. Isn't the Jesus Prayer a mantra?

No, it is not. The Jesus Prayer is an ancient prayer from the Christian East. Similarly to the stages of western forms of mental prayer that are enumerated in this book, the Jesus Prayer unfolds in stages (see **Question 82**). In the first stage, you pray orally, "Lord Jesus Christ, Son of God, have mercy on me, a sinner." This practice corresponds to vocal prayer. Then you move on to praying it mentally (mental prayer). The third stage is called *the prayer of the heart.* It corresponds with what the Carmelite saints and the western Church call *infused contemplation.* [103]

Both the Hindu mantra and the Jesus Prayer are repetitive, and both are seen as means of union with the deity of a particular religion. But there are many important differences, including:

- The Jesus Prayer uses words to cry out to a personal God who is eternally Other. A mantra uses words to reach an altered state of consciousness, and finally a merging of the self into the "Ultimate Reality."

- The Jesus Prayer is intimately connected with conversion. A mantra is simply a technique.

- The Jesus Prayer contains the Gospel in miniature. A mantra can be complete nonsense, or use the names of false gods, and still "work."

---

[103] "Three Stages in the Practice of the Jesus Prayer," *Orthodox-Prayer.org,*
https://www.orthodoxprayer.org/Jesus%20Prayer/Jesus%20Prayer-Three%20Stages.html. Accessed 5/31/19.

- The Jesus Prayer makes our Lord the focus. A mantra puts oneself in control.[104]

76. *What is Centering Prayer?*

For this answer, I quote from my book *Is Centering Prayer Catholic?*[105]

> Centering Prayer was created by Fr. Thomas Keating, Fr. Basil Pennington, and Fr. William Meninger. In the 1970s they were all monks at the Trappist monastery in Spencer, Massachusetts. Fr. Keating was the abbot. After inviting Zen Buddhists and Transcendental Meditation masters to dialog and lead retreats, they looked for a way to bridge the gap between Christianity and eastern religious practice. Their goal was to find a way to reach out to people who were interested in eastern meditation and bring them into the Catholic faith instead. Then Fr. Meninger read *The Cloud of Unknowing,* a book about deep prayer by an anonymous fourteenth-century English author. Looking at it through the influence of the eastern meditation techniques presented at the monastery, he misunderstood it, thinking the author was advocating a similar practice. He began to teach a new form of prayer, which

---

[104] Dionysios Farasiotis, "The Jesus Prayer and the Hindu Mantra," OrthodoxPrayer.org, http://www.orthodoxprayer.org/Articles_files/Farasiotis-JesusPrayer-HinduMantra.html Accessed 5/31/19.
[105] You can purchase *Is Centering Prayer Catholic?* at major online bookstores. It is on Amazon in paperback and ebook at https://www.amazon.com/dp/0997202335/.

he called the Prayer of the Cloud. Fr. Keating later applied the term Centering Prayer, adapted from the writings of Thomas Merton, to this new prayer form.

In practicing Centering Prayer, a person begins with the intent of entering God's presence. Then he sits quietly, trying to ignore all thoughts, feelings, and impressions for the length of the prayer time. When thoughts or feelings take hold, he gently repeats a 'sacred word,' chosen ahead of time. This word is meant to signify his intent to be open to God's action. The period ends with a few minutes of reorienting himself to daily life, returning from a deeper state of consciousness. Centering Prayer is supposed to give modern Catholics a taste of being receptive to God.

There are numerous problems with Centering Prayer, both in the practice itself and in the theology that is taught along with it. Please see **Questions 77-80.**

77. How is Centering Prayer problematic?

The website of Fr. William Meninger says:

In 1974, Father William Meninger... found a dusty little book in the abbey library, *The Cloud of Unknowing.* As he read it, he was delighted to discover that this anonymous 14th century book presented contemplative meditation as a teachable, spiritual process enabling the ordinary person to enter and receive a direct experience of union with God.

> This form of meditation, recently known as "Centering Prayer" ... can be traced from and through the earliest centuries of Christianity. The Centering Prayer centers one on God....
>
> He quickly began teaching contemplative prayer according to *The Cloud of Unknowing* at the Abbey Retreat House.[106]

This statement showcases many of the problems with the Centering Prayer movement:

- The lack of consistency in defining what expression of prayer Centering Prayer is. Is it meditation, "meditative contemplation," or contemplative prayer itself?
- Offering the teaching of *The Cloud of Unknowing* to all, when the author warns it is meant for a select few who are not beginners in prayer.
- Mistaking a suggested response to God's supernatural intervention for a method of attaining that intervention.
- Thinking contemplative prayer is "teachable" through a set of steps.

Besides this, Centering Prayer advocates teach that you should turn away from all thoughts during prayer, "even the most devout thoughts."[107] They confuse God's presence in the soul by nature of his role of Creator and Sustainer of

---

[106] https://contemplativeprayer.net/. Some punctuation edited for clarity. Accessed 5/3/19.

[107] Fr. Thomas Keating, *Open Mind, Open Heart* (London: Continuum, 2006), 21.

all that exists, and union with God through grace. They teach religious indifferentism (the idea that one religion is as good as another), if not syncretism (mixing practices and beliefs of various religions). Those who practice meditation in other religions are said to have the same goals as contemplative Christians and are supposedly able to attain those goals.[108] They distort the darkness of the contemplative life (see **Questions 93-96**), equating it with neither knowing nor wanting to know who or what God is.[109] In Centering Prayer, Jesus is relegated to a teacher, who is barely mentioned. Ignorance and psychological wounds replace sin as the central human problem. Panentheism[110] is invoked in a failed attempt to shake off the accusation of pantheistic teachings.

Fr. Keating has said,

> The beginning of the spiritual journey is the realization that there is a Higher Power or God, or to make it as easy as possible for everybody, that there is an Other; Capital O. Second step: to try to become the Other; still a Capital O. And finally, the realization that there IS no Other; you and the Other are One.

---

[108] Kess Frey, *Bridge across Troubled Waters: Centering Prayer and the Theological Divide* (Great Barrington, MA: Lindisfarne, 2017), 99, 104.

[109] Keating, *Open Mind* 41 and 66.

[110] *The Stanford Encyclopedia of Philosophy* explains that panentheism is an attempt to find a middle ground between a theistic view that sees God as only transcendent, and a pantheistic view that sees God as only immanent. However, panentheism has no fixed set of beliefs. "Panentheism," http://plato.stanford.edu/entries/panentheism/, February 5, 2103 (accessed July 10, 2015).

Always have been, always will be. You just think
that you aren't.[111]

This is not a Christian conception of God.

All these problems and more are documented in my
book, *Is Centering Prayer Catholic?*

78. Did Teresa of Ávila suggest something like Centering Prayer?

Just as they do with *The Cloud of Unknowing,* teachers of
problematic modern prayer methods misinterpret Teresa's
teaching. She taught that someone who is experiencing early forms of contemplation can say a word or phrase of love
now and then to keep his mind from wandering. Her teaching was very close to that of *The Cloud of Unknowing* on this
point. Neither one advocates using a word or phrase to
change your state of consciousness or to prepare yourself
for contemplation. In fact, Teresa says:

> Taking it upon oneself to stop and suspend thought
> is what I mean should not be done; nor should we
> cease to work with the intellect, because otherwise
> we would be left like cold simpletons and be doing
> neither one thing nor the other. When the Lord sus-
> pends the intellect and causes it to stop, He Himself
> gives it that which holds its attention and makes it
> marvel and without reflection it understands more
> in the space of a Creed than we can understand with

---

[111] Fr. Thomas Keating, "You and the Other (with a Capital O),"
ONE, YouTube Video, 1:21, posted by Bill Ramos, July 8, 2008,
https://www.youtube.com/watch?v=Rd2LPjpd9As.

all our earthly diligence in many years. Trying to keep the soul's faculties busy and thinking you can make them be quiet is foolish.[112]

In Centering Prayer, you are instructed to ignore all thoughts, feelings, and inspirations in prayer. It directly contradicts Saint Teresa's teaching. It also contradicts the teaching of John of the Cross on when you should put aside meditating on Scripture. John wrote:

> At the proper time one should abandon this imaginative meditation so that the journey to God may not be hindered, but so that there is no regression, one should not abandon it before the due time ... as long as one can make discursive meditation and draw out satisfaction, one must not abandon this method.[113]

You must continue to meditate on Sacred Scripture until you observe the three signs that God is leading you into

---

[112] *The Life of St. Teresa of Jesus* Chap. 12, 8-9. One Centering Prayer practitioner has challenged me on this point by claiming that you *can* take it upon yourself to stop your thoughts, provided you are at the right stage. This is clearly contrary to Saint Teresa's meaning. As John of the Cross shows, one of the primary signs that you are ready to stop meditating is that you find it virtually impossible to meditate. It is "the Lord [who] suspends the intellect." You can only cooperate with his work.

[113] *Ascent of Mt. Carmel* 2, 13. Centering Prayer practitioners try to get around this teaching by continuing to practice Lectio divina outside of their Centering Prayer time. Thus, they can claim they have not "abandoned" meditation. This is an obvious subversion of John's teaching. He never envisioned practicing meditation separately from one's contemplation in the same stage of life.

contemplation (see **Question 110**). To do otherwise is to risk going backwards rather than forwards.

For a more detailed analysis of the problems with Centering Prayer, see my book, *Is Centering Prayer Catholic?*

79. What has the Church said about eastern meditation?

In 1989 the Congregation for the Doctrine of the Faith (CDF) issued the authoritative document *On Some Aspects of Christian Meditation.* What was the purpose of the document?

> The ever more frequent contact with other religions and with their different styles and methods of prayer has, in recent decades, led many of the faithful to ask themselves what value non-Christian forms of meditation might have for Christians. Above all, the question concerns eastern methods.... Observing that in recent times many traditional methods of meditation, especially Christian ones, have fallen into disuse, they wonder whether it might not now be possible, by a new training in prayer, to enrich our heritage by incorporating what has until now been foreign to it.[114]

The first footnote mentions techniques found in Hinduism and Buddhism, and more specifically, Zen, Transcendental Meditation, and Yoga. About foreign religions, the CDF says, "One can take from them what is useful so long as the Christian conception of prayer, its logic and requirements are never obscured."[115] Several examples of com-

---

[114] *On Some Aspects of Christian Meditation* no.2.
[115] Ibid. no 16.

monalities or borrowing are given in the following paragraphs: eastern religions, like Christians since ancient times, value spiritual masters; the idea of the three stages of the spiritual life (see **Question 83**) came from non-Christian sources; and there is some legitimacy in using "the position and demeanor of the body" to aid recollection.[116] But the CDF goes into great detail about how these beliefs and practices were Christianized and refined.

A person could go too far by appropriating wholesale beliefs and practices incompatible with the Faith. Some of the errors the CDF warns against are:

- Seeing the material world as evil.

- Thinking that desolation (see **Question 50**) is a sign that the Holy Spirit has abandoned you.

- Rejecting the use of the senses and the intellect in prayer.

- A "negative" theology that turns away from the truths taught in the Scriptures.

- Rejection of the "very idea of the One and Triune God, who is Love, in favor of an immersion 'in the indeterminate abyss of the divinity.'"[117]

- Remaining "in oneself," rather than moving from self toward God.[118]

- Relying on technique in order to grow in union with God.

---

[116] Ibid. no. 26.
[117] *On Some Aspects of Christian Meditation* no. 12.
[118] Ibid. no. 19.

- Interpreting the natural euphoria that comes from some exercises (such as Yoga) as the action of the Holy Spirit.

Returning to the positive, the CDF notes that it is possible for some meditative practices from both the Christian and non-Christian East to be used as a pacifying preparation for prayer. However, one must take into account all the warnings of the document. The CDF does not give specifics about which practices it has in mind here, but from the larger context it appears to be speaking about such practices as focusing on one's breath or heartbeat, as eastern Christians have done. Again, this is only speaking of immediate preparation for prayer. The CDF is not referring to practicing these techniques for long periods each day, separate from one's prayer time or as a substitute for prayer.

Pope John Paul II also addressed Buddhism in *Crossing the Threshold of Hope.* He said:

> It is not inappropriate to caution those Christians who enthusiastically welcome certain ideas originating in the religious traditions of the Far East — for example, techniques and methods of meditation and ascetical practice. In some quarters these have become fashionable, and are accepted rather uncritically. First one should know one's own spiritual heritage well and consider whether it is right to set it aside lightly.[119]

---

[119] Pope John Paul II, *Crossing the Threshold of Hope* (NY: Knopf, 1994), 89-90. Emphasis in the original.

80. Has the Church addressed Centering Prayer or the use of mantras?

As noted in answer to **Question 74**, the document *Jesus Christ, Bearer of the Water of Life: A Christian Reflection on the 'New Age'* does mention mantras. However, some Catholic practitioners of eastern meditation dismiss this document, since it lacks magisterial authority. It is working document created by the Pontifical Councils on Culture and Interreligious Dialogue.

The authoritative document *On Some Aspects of Christian Meditation* appears to refer to the mantra-meditation of Fr. John Main, as well as Centering Prayer (without naming them) in this passage:

> With the present diffusion of eastern methods of meditation in the Christian world and in ecclesial communities, we find ourselves faced with a pointed renewal of an attempt, which is not free from dangers and errors, *to fuse Christian meditation with that which is non-Christian.* Proposals in this direction are numerous and radical to a greater or lesser extent. Some use eastern methods solely as a psycho-physical preparation for a truly Christian contemplation; others go further and, using different techniques, try to generate spiritual experiences similar to those described in the writings of certain Catholic mystics.[120]

---

[120] *On Some Aspects of Christian Meditation* no. 12. Emphasis in the original.

The footnote on this passage reads, "See, for example, *The Cloud of Unknowing*, a spiritual work by an anonymous English writer of the fourteenth century."[121] Both Fr. Main and Fr. Thomas Keating of the Centering Prayer movement point to *The Cloud of Unknowing* as the origin or confirmation of their methods. They do teach that through their methods one can experience what the Catholic mystics wrote about.

In my book *Is Centering Prayer Catholic?* I show how several other teachings of *On Some Aspects of Christian Meditation* apply to Centering Prayer. Most of them would apply equally well to Fr. Main's "Christian Meditation." The fact that the CDF document fails to mention these men or their movements by name is irrelevant. It does not address *any* modern prayer form or teacher by name; rather, it gives general guidelines to the world's bishops about problematic practices that each should apply to the specific situation in his diocese.

81. Is Yoga an acceptable practice?

In the document *On Some Aspects of Christian Meditation,* the Congregation for the Doctrine of the Faith (CDF) addressed the use of bodily positions and physical exercise in prayer:

> Some physical exercises automatically produce a feeling of quiet and relaxation, pleasing sensations, perhaps even phenomena of light and of warmth, which resemble spiritual well-being. To take such feelings for the authentic consolations of the Holy Spirit would be a totally erroneous way of conceiving the spiritual life. Giving them a symbolic signifi-

---

[121] Ibid. Footnote 13.

cance typical of the mystical experience, when the moral condition of the person concerned does not correspond to such an experience, would represent a kind of mental schizophrenia which could also lead to psychic disturbance and, at times, to moral deviations.[122]

The Church here notes that practices like Yoga, presumably even if they are done purely for exercise, can lead you to think that God is somehow touching you. The danger is real. According to an article in *Psychology Today,* more than 90 percent of those who take up Yoga do so simply for exercise. Two-thirds of them change their motive after beginning Yoga, most often continuing for the sake of "spiritual benefit or self-actualization."[123] In Catholic circles, one author styles herself as the Catholic Yogi, seeing her Yoga practice as prayer. Others teach or promote "Ignatian Yoga," in which groups are led through Yoga poses in front of the Tabernacle. Needless to say, Yoga is not in line with the teaching of Saint Ignatius, and Yoga is not Christian prayer.

The CDF reminds us that the Christian life is one of conversion. Yoga and similar practices can make you feel spiritual, even as if you are experiencing deep prayer, when you may actually be living a life of sin. That's because these practices are geared toward the feeling of oneness with God or the universe.

---

[122] *On Some Aspects of Christian Meditation* no. 28.
[123] Marlynn Wei, MD, "Why Does Anyone Do Yoga, Anyway?" *Psychology Today.*
https://www.psychologytoday.com/us/blog/-urban-survival/201506/why-does-anyone-do-yoga-anyway. Accessed 5/31/19.

Yoga is a Hindu practice, a Hindu meditation technique. Like other forms of eastern meditation, it is not compatible with growth in Christian prayer.[124]

---

[124] The Church has not addressed the issue of Yoga stretches that have been stripped of the accompanying breathing techniques, chants, et cetera, that make it meditation.

The Different Stages of Christian Prayer

82. *What are the nine grades of prayer?*

The nine grades of prayer follow Saint Teresa of Ávila's teaching on prayer growth in *Interior Castle*. One normally progresses through them in order, although adjacent grades blend into each other, and sometimes the soul needs to return to a lower grade of prayer for a time. You should never try to skip ahead, but let the Holy Spirit lead you from one grade to the next. Grades one through four are active, prayers you can make with the help of ordinary actual grace. Grades five and above are contemplation, which means you cannot attain them by your efforts.

1. Vocal prayer.

2. Discursive meditation.

3. Affective prayer.

4. Acquired recollection. Also known as the prayer of simplicity or simple gaze.

5. Infused recollection.

6. Prayer of quiet.

7. (Simple) union.

8. Spiritual betrothal. Also known as Conforming union.

9. Spiritual marriage. Also known as Transforming union.

83. What are the three stages of the spiritual life?

Spiritual writers of the early centuries, led by an author known as Pseudo-Dionysius, recognized that the spiritual life unfolds in three stages. These stages are known as the purgative way, the illuminative way, and the unitive way.

The purgative way is the stage of beginners. Most Christians spend much or all of their lives in this stage. In the purgative way, you practice mental prayer, try to overcome habitual sin, and do light penances. (*Habitual sin* means any sin that you commit deliberately, especially in a habitual manner. It indicates an attachment to sin that is not compatible with union with God. Sins of passion or those committed without full knowledge or some consent of the will are excluded from this term.) The soul in the purgative way operates with common actual grace. Fr. Reginald Garrigou-Lagrange and other authors liken this stage to spiritual childhood.

The illuminative way begins with what Saint John of the Cross calls the passive night of the senses (see **Question 93**). This is a dark, dry contemplation. In other words, the soul experiences no consolation in the senses (see **Question 49**). God is working in a hidden manner that bewilders the soul and makes meditation difficult. This stage purges you from your pride and your attachment to the material world. It teaches you how weak you are and how you can truly make no advances in the spiritual life except by God's help. After this dry transition period, most people experience a delightful contemplation as their norm for years. (That does not mean they never experience dryness or desolation.) As prayer deepens, some may experience phenomena such as ecstasies, visions, and even levitation! This stage has been likened to spiritual adolescence.

Then God initiates a further passive purgation known as the dark night of the spirit.[125] This night is extremely painful. Saints compare it to Purgatory or even hell. When the soul emerges from this night, she enters the unitive way, in which God brings her to the transforming union.[126] This stage is like spiritual adulthood.

84. What are the different levels of meditative prayer?

Discursive prayer is another name for meditation. Discursive describes applying your reasoning powers to prayer. It is

---

[125] Both dark nights also have an active component. That is, before God initiates the passive nights, you must actively work on detaching yourself from sensory or spiritual things, depending on your stage of growth.

[126] Various authorities place the passive night of the spirit before or after the spiritual betrothal, or before, during, or after what Saint Teresa calls the sixth mansions. The discrepancy probably derives from the fact that Teresa does not talk about the nights as a separate stage. Also, many people enter the passive nights slowly and gradually, rather than all at once. A similar disagreement exists over whether the first passive night is part of the third or fourth mansions. I like to think of the passive nights as a bridge between mansions, not fully in one or the next.

related to the word *discourse.* Many people confine their use of the word *meditation* to speaking about discursive meditation. But if you think of meditation as prayer that begins with stimulating the senses — including the five physical senses, the memory, and the imagination — you can then divide meditation into three stages.

The second stage of meditation is usually called *affective prayer,* and the third has many names, including *acquired recollection* and the *prayer of simplicity.*

Affective prayer is the prayer of the heart (will), while discursive meditation is the prayer of the mind (intellect). Fr. Jordan Aumann, OP, says, "The most important element in meditation is the act of love aroused in the will on the presentation of some supernatural truth by the intellect."[127]

Saint Teresa agrees:

> For mental prayer in my opinion is nothing else than an intimate sharing between friends; it means taking time frequently to be alone with him who we know loves us. The important thing is not to think much but to love much and so do that which best stirs you to love. Love is not great delight but desire to please God in everything.[128]

When you have practiced meditation for some time (although this can also happen with beginners) you tend to move quickly from the mind to the will within your prayer time. Instead of lots of reasoning, you are drawn toward speaking lovingly to Christ. This is exactly as it should be.

---

[127] *Spiritual Theology* 2, 12.
[128] *Interior Castle* 4, 2.

Fr. Aumann gives several pieces of practical advice regarding affective prayer:

- You need material to feed the mind before the will is moved (a book, a picture, a mental image).
- Don't run from one movement of the will to another.
- Gently return to discursive meditation when the affections have run their course.
- Be careful of confusing affective prayer with infused contemplation (see the section **Contemplative Prayer**).
- Don't get lazy with discursive meditation.
- Keep your focus on God, not the sweetness of your prayer.

More details on acquired recollection are given in *The Way of Perfection*. Saint Teresa writes:

> But if we cultivate the habit, make the necessary effort and practice the exercises [of recollecting ourselves] for several days, the benefits will reveal themselves, and when we begin to pray we shall realize that the bees are coming to the hive and entering it to make the honey, and all without any effort of ours. For it is the Lord's will that, in return for the time which their efforts have cost them, the soul and the will should be given this power over the senses. They will only have to make a sign to show that they wish to enter into recollection and the senses will obey and allow themselves to be recollected. Later they may come out again, but it is a great thing that they should ever have surrendered,

for if they come out it is as captives and slaves and they do none of the harm that they might have done before.[129]

When you first begin a life of prayer, meditation is difficult. Then it becomes easier. Before long, you find yourself moving toward more affective prayer. After some time, often a few years or more, a further simplification of prayer occurs. Now, instead of being moved to speak to Jesus, you are moved by your meditation to sit quietly in his presence. As Saint Teresa says, this gaze of love may last only a few seconds. Then you return to your image or reflection, until recollection occurs again. At times the recollection may last for several minutes. Or you may sit quietly for an hour, with just a glance now and then back at the image that first helped you recollect yourself. Your prayer time flies by. It is sweet, and you try to make more time for prayer if your duties allow it. God is preparing your soul for the gift of infused contemplation.

When you begin to experience this, you should give yourself up to it. You should never force yourself to meditate or to speak. On the other hand, you should not try to unnaturally prolong acquired recollection, nor leave discursive meditation completely behind at this point. You should always begin prayer with something concrete and let the Holy Spirit move you as he wills to affective prayer or recollection.

---

[129] *Way of Perfection* Chap. 28.

85. What are the four waters of prayer?

In *The Book of Her Life,* Teresa of Ávila spoke of four levels or degrees of prayer, using the analogy of four different ways of watering a garden.[130]

1. Drawing water from a well. This is the active prayer of the purgative way, meditation. Prayer takes lots of effort at this stage.

2. Turning the crank on a water wheel and using aqueducts. You still need to put forth an effort, but prayer is easier than in the first stage and brings more dramatic results. This is infused recollection and the prayer of quiet.

3. Letting water from a river or stream flow into the garden. The gardener has to do some work, but mostly reaps the benefit of past work. This is the prayer of union.

4. Rain. This level of prayer requires no effort at all. Here prayer overwhelms the senses in what is known as rapture or ecstasy. The spiritual betrothal and spiritual marriage are at this fourth level.

In her later works, particularly *Interior Castle,* Teresa had a better understanding of the different stages of prayer and how each was different from the next. Instead of dividing the spiritual life into four waters, she divided it into seven groups of mansions. Some of her teaching about each level was refined. The water analogy gives a good mental picture

---

[130] *Life* Chap. 11. The details of each stage are given in chapters 11 to 21.

of different degrees of prayer, but the analogy of the mansions is the more authoritative understanding.

86. How do Saint Teresa's mansions correlate with the grades of prayer?

In her most famous and most mature book, *Interior Castle*, Saint Teresa of Ávila uses the image of rooms in a castle for stages of spiritual growth. She writes:

> I began to think of the soul as if it were a castle made of a single diamond or of very clear crystal, in which there are many rooms, just as in Heaven there are many mansions....

> Let us now imagine that this castle, as I have said, contains many mansions, some above, others below, others at each side; and in the centre and midst of them all is the chiefest mansion where the most secret things pass between God and the soul.[131]

Teresa divides the spiritual journey into seven mansions or groups of mansions. She says that the divisions between these mansions are not strict. One stage blends into the next. Nor do you necessarily go straight through from mansions one to seven. Instead, there is much wandering in and out of various stages. Still, she advises readers on what they should expect at different stages and what to work on.

The first three mansions are in the purgative way (see **Question 83**). The illuminative way contains mansions four

---

[131] *Interior Castle* 1, 1.

and five. Mansions six and seven comprise the unitive way.[132]

Teresa does not speak much about the prayer of those in the purgative way. She does, however, mention both vocal prayer and mental prayer. She teaches elsewhere that meditation is necessary for spiritual growth.[133] She also speaks about acquired recollection, which is an active prayer. Discalced Carmelites (that is, those who belong to the branch of the Carmelite order founded by Teresa and John of the Cross) generally relate the mansions to the different grades or stages of prayer as in the following diagram. The diagram also includes the passive nights that John speaks about (what most people mean by "the dark night of the soul;" see **Question 93**). In this diagram, the passive nights act as bridges between different stages, beginning in one and ending in the next.

---

[132] I am giving the division in accordance with Carmelite sources, as they seem to agree best with Saints John and Teresa. Other authorities, particularly Fr. Reginald Garrigou-Lagrange, correlate the mansions with the three ways of the interior life in a slightly different manner.

[133] *Way of Perfection* Chap. 16.

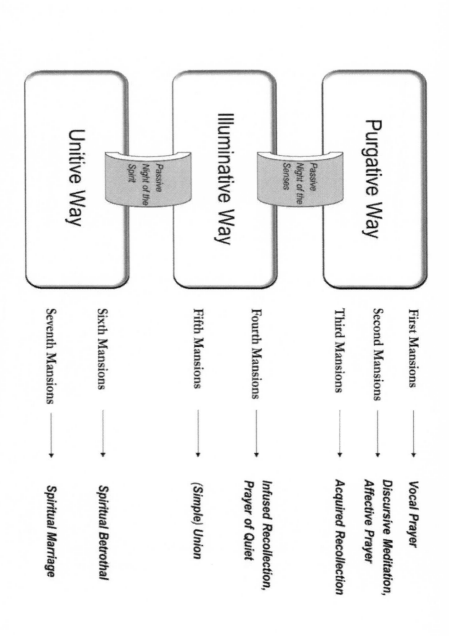

87. *Should I know what spiritual stage I am in?*

This is a common question that is oddly controversial. Often, people argue that you should not be "obsessed" with where you are at. Well, you should not be obsessed with anything, because that is opposed to loving God with your whole heart, mind, and soul. But knowing or having a reasonable assurance about something is not the same as being obsessed with it.

Teresa of Ávila was asked to write *Interior Castle* to help people know what to expect and how to act as they grow closer to God. John of the Cross identified ignorance as one of the main reasons people fail to advance.[134]

If you have a good spiritual director, and he or she understands what stage you are at and can direct you accordingly, you are relieved of some of the burden of understanding spiritual stages. If you are at the stage of transition from meditation to contemplation, it is especially important to receive correct advice on how to pray. A good director will pick up on the signs that you are in this transition and tell you when to begin being more passive in prayer. See **Question 117** on the importance of spiritual directors.

It is less important to know whether your prayer is mainly the prayer of quiet or of union, for example. And being able to pinpoint the exact one of Teresa's mansions you are in is not necessary. In fact, even Teresa herself said that the dividing lines between one mansion and another were not sharp.

Some people believe that knowledge of their spiritual state will make them proud. But anyone who lacks humility has probably not progressed beyond the purgative way. And

---

[134] *Ascent of Mt. Carmel* Prologue.

if you are still in the purgative way, you are still in the childhood stage of the spiritual life. There is nothing for you to be proud of, since you have barely begun to live for God. In fact, knowing you are only in the second of the seven mansions, for example, can increase your humility and self-knowledge. It can inspire you to work harder, to give God more. With the limited self-knowledge of the purgative way, people often think they are nearly saints just because they are trying to follow God more than they perceive the average person to be doing.

If after some study you cannot discern what stage you are at, and you lack a spiritual director who can help you do so, don't fixate on the question. Just make a reasonable effort to understand your state and calmly act as you believe the Lord is asking you to.

88. Will I ever really leave the purgative way?

Purgation is not equivalent to the purgative way. The purgative way is a particular stage identified by Christians of the early centuries and accepted by saints and theologians ever since. This is the stage of beginners. In this stage, you actively work to purge yourself from mortal sin and habitual venial sin. Then God begins purging you of attachments on the level of the exterior senses, the imagination, and the sense memory. When the intensity of this purgation is over, you have left the purgative way behind.

Purgation itself, however, continues. You must continue to give up sins that you did not recognize in the past. You must work toward detachment from all spiritual goods, clinging to God alone. God then will initiate the second passive night, with further infused purgation. This night will complete any unfinished purgation of the senses and the spirit. Once you have passed through this night, no further purgation is required. You are ready to enter heaven. However, some saints suffer for others' sake (as victim souls), even at the height of the spiritual life (see **Question 98**). And some souls, such as Saint Teresa of Calcutta, experience darkness until their death, even though they are in union with God. This experience is rarer.

89. What signs mark the end of the purgative way?

In order to leave the purgative way, you need to overcome deliberate sin, even venial sin. You will still commit sins of passion or realize after committing an act that it was objectively sinful. There may also be some sins related to your temperament that you have difficulty conquering. You will rarely if ever consciously choose to sin, because your love for God is becoming more and more of a priority. The other preparation for leaving the purgative way is experiencing acquired recollection (see **Question 84**).

You should not assume you are at this stage without advice from an objective and knowledgeable person, preferably a spiritual director. Most people misunderstand what this stage entails.

Please see **Question 110** on the transition from meditation to contemplation for further information.

Advancing in Prayer

90. How can I tell if I am making progress?

Spiritual progress should be measurable, but at the beginning it may come slowly. Here are some ideas for measuring growth:

- Keep a spiritual journal with your failures, triumphs, and a summary of your prayer time.
- Go to Confession at least once a month.
- Do a daily examination of conscience.
- Seek spiritual direction and ask your director for help.

In addition, Saint Francis de Sales and others advise to focus on only one virtue at a time.[135] It is much easier to see your progress if you have a narrow focus to your spiritual life.

Regarding making progress in prayer specifically, mental prayer is usually difficult at first. With practice, it becomes easier and even enjoyable. Over time, if you continue to surrender to God, your prayer should become simpler without your having to force the process. The natural simplification of prayer is a good sign that you are progressing.

---

[135] See, for example, *Introduction to the Devout Life* 3, 1.

91. Sometimes I feel moved to just silently adore God. Is this okay?

It's not only okay, it's a higher form of prayer than discursive meditation. This is acquired recollection or the prayer of simple gaze (see **Question 84**).

Watch out for the following errors regarding acquired recollection. The first is being afraid of this simplification of prayer and filling the stillness with words. Doing so stifles the Holy Spirit and stunts growth. The opposite error is giving yourself completely up to silence, abandoning meditation. This practice cultivates spiritual gluttony, making you attached to the consolations of prayer. A third error, prominent in our day, is trying to achieve recollection through mental techniques. Techniques can produce a mental silence, but it is the result of a manipulation that is incompatible with deep prayer. Real growth must be accompanied by ever-deepening conversion. The final error is to take this prayer for infused contemplation, which is a pure gift. Acquired recollection is still an active prayer, even though simplified. (See the section **Contemplative Prayer**.)

At this stage you should still begin each time of mental prayer with Scripture, returning to a simple idea from your reading or to the written word itself when the silence fails or your mind wanders. Strive more than ever to live a life of virtue and love of neighbor. Doing these two things will keep you moving forward, preparing you for the gift of contemplation.

92. Is the prayer of recollection the same as practicing the presence of God?

Recollection can be acquired (produced by human activity) or infused (given by God). In acquired recollection, you bring yourself into God's presence and fix your attention upon him in a simple manner. You can do this within your mental prayer, in which case you are practicing the prayer of simple gaze. Or you can recall your mind to the thought of God and express your love for him without words as you go throughout the day. In this case, you are practicing the presence of God.

In infused recollection, you find yourself gazing on God without necessarily having done anything immediate to make this happen. Infused recollection can also occur outside of prayer, although it is more common during mental prayer. See **Question 109** for more on the different types of recollection.

93. What is the dark night of the soul?

This is one of the most difficult questions to answer! Let's break it down into several sections.

1. **Terminology:** John of the Cross, who coined the term, actually speaks of two nights, the night of the senses and the night of the spirit. Each of them has an active component (what you can do with ordinary grace to purge yourself) and an infused component (accomplished by God).

2. **Preparation:** A prerequisite of the passive night of the senses is overcoming habitual sin of all kinds (see **Question 89**). You must do all you can with ordinary grace to draw

near to God before he draws near to you in contempla-tion.[136]

3. Timing: The passive night of the senses marks the transi-tion from the purgative to the illuminative way (see **Question 83**). Some authors place it in the third mansions, others in the fourth. Picture it as spanning the two (see the diagram with **Question 86**). The passive night of the spirit marks the transition to the unitive way and is usually placed in the sixth mansions.

4. **What are these nights?** They are a necessary, progres-sive cleansing that prepares you for greater union with God. In the first night, the night of the senses, God detaches you from your exterior senses, imagination, and sense memory. (The sense memory refers to those things you have stored in your mind that you experienced through your senses — things you saw, heard, tasted, and so on. You can also store purely spiritual experiences in the mind. This aspect of the memory is cleansed in the second night.) In the second, the night of the spirit, he detaches you from your clinging to spiritual things. The nights are infused, a contemplation that begins without consolation (see **Question 40**), but usu-ally turns sweet.

5. **What happens in prayer during the passive nights?** You reach the passive night of the senses after you have been experiencing acquired recollection — a consoling and simple form of meditation (see **Question 84**). Now you have trouble meditating at all. It seems like there is a mental

---

[136] See Jas 4:8.

block or that Scripture is meaningless. Prayer is dry. Distractions abound. You feel drawn to sit in silence, but receive no consolation in doing so. You fear you are doing nothing, just sitting idle. God has to make it impossible — or at least very difficult — for you to meditate, so that you will get out of the way and let him work. At the same time or soon afterward, you begin seeing your sinfulness at a new level. It seems that you are moving backward instead of forward. Patient perseverance and careful carrying out of God's will are the keys to advancing. The passive night of the spirit is similar, but more intense. (Of course, the problems with meditating are irrelevant by this point, because you would not have been trying to meditate for a long time before reaching the second passive night.) Many people who go through this latter night feel like they are tasting hell.

94. How is the passive night different from ordinary dryness?

Sometimes it is difficult to tell the difference between the two, especially when you are just entering the passive night. Only a good spiritual director can tell you for certain whether your dryness comes from God's action in your soul or more ordinary causes. However, you can ask yourself:

- Am I over-tired?
- Am I sick?
- Am I anxious or preoccupied?
- Am I being lazy in prayer?
- Have I fallen into sin or drawn back from God?

- Am I praying at a time or in a place that is not conducive to prayer?

If you can answer *no* to all those questions, then it is *possible* you are in the passive night. (Conversely, mental or physical health problems often accompany the passive night, so you could answer *yes* to a few of the questions and still be in the passive night.) The passive night usually starts gradually, but the dryness should be enduring and become more frequent. Dryness that clears up when you get more sleep, feel better physically, or are less anxious probably stems from natural causes. The dryness of the passive night often continues for years, requiring patient perseverance and an increase of faith in God's hidden presence.

The passive night will increase your desire for God, decrease your dependence on any consolations you receive in prayer, and give you the grace to follow God more faithfully than ever before. You should also expect to receive more insight into the state of your soul. If these signs are absent, you are likely in spiritual desolation rather than the passive night (see **Question 50**).

95. How is the dark night different from other kinds of suffering?

Suffering comes to everyone as a result of Original Sin. God can bring good out of every kind of suffering, if you allow him to. In the spiritual life, however, there is a particular suffering that is caused by a change in your relationship with God. John of the Cross calls this suffering a dark night (see **Question 93**).

In the active night of the senses, which begins when you make a firm decision to put God first, you work to turn away from sin and toward God. This change causes suffering, as you must give up deep-rooted habits of selfishness. When you have done all you can to purge yourself from sin, God initiates the passive night of the senses. He purifies you on the level of the senses by taking away the consolation you have enjoyed in prayer. He makes meditation difficult or impossible, so that you learn that deeper prayer is pure grace, your efforts being useless to attain it. He also shows you your sinfulness on a new level. Just when you were thinking that you had conquered sin, you learn that you have barely begun to do so. Difficulties and dryness in prayer and greater self-knowledge are what causes the pain of this night, especially for those who fear that they have offended God and have been abandoned by him. Those who persevere in prayer and follow God's will as closely as possible will eventually exit this passive night and enjoy the peaceful and delightful prayer of quiet.

Beginning with the first passive night, you must practice the active night of the spirit, continuing to root out previously unrecognized sins and detaching yourself from even the greatest spiritual goods. This activity continues in the delightful contemplation of the illuminative way. When you have done all you can in this active night, God again draws you closer through the passive night of the spirit. He purges you from attachment to absolutely everything except himself. The pain goes deeper than one who has not experienced it can imagine. At the end of this night, you are ready to see God face to face.

In short, the pain of the dark nights comes as a result of God's action. He can use ordinary suffering to purge you to some extent, and many people experience physical or mental difficulties while going through the passive nights. However, ordinary suffering is only *allowed* by God. The passive nights are *caused* by God for your good.

96. What is a "dark desire" in prayer?

Dark desire means a desire for God that cannot be put into words. You thirst for God, but nothing you say, think, feel, or imagine can adequately express your thirst. One of the primary effects of the passive night of the senses is an exponential increase in this desire. At times, even though you believe you desire union with God with all your heart, you are unable to *feel* any desire in prayer. Thus, it is dark, hidden from the soul.

John of the Cross similarly speaks of the passive night of the senses as *dark contemplation.*[137] The soul is blinded and bewildered. Closeness to Jesus becomes a matter of faith rather than sight. You cannot understand what is happening, whether the Holy Spirit is really working in your soul or you are deceiving yourself. Dark contemplation causes a growth in detachment, humility, and patience. You learn to rely on God alone, as you cannot even make yourself feel any emotion while in prayer, or think two consecutive, meaningful thoughts about the Scripture you have read.

97. How can I work on the active night of the senses?

In the active night of the senses (see **Questions 93-95**), you detach first of all from mortal sin, then from venial sin, then from anything on the sense level that you use in an inordinate manner. You follow the commandments, the

---

[137] *Ascent of Mt. Carmel* Prologue.

teachings of the Church, and the Beatitudes. You perform small extra penances such as you might do during Lent. (See also **Question 98** regarding mortification.) At the same time, you work on specific virtues, one by one. Both of these aspects of the active night (mortification and practicing virtue) are essential training for the passive night. When you don't know what else to work on, ask the Holy Spirit, "What do I still lack?" Having removed the large barriers to God, you will be more sensitive to the little things. If God seems to make you wait for the passive night, be patient and humble. God will come to you when the time is right.

98. How should mortification change as I advance in prayer?

People often equate mortification solely with bodily penance, but mortification is any act in which you die to yourself for love of Christ. Fr. John Hardon writes:

> The best description of mortification was given by Our Lord. He said to His disciples, "If anyone wishes to come after me, let him deny himself and take up his cross and follow me" (Mat 16:24).
>
> Mortification, therefore, is self-denial. And self-denial is doing the will of God, even when the Divine will crosses at right angles to our will. Mortification is the imitation of Christ in the surrender of what we naturally like in order to please God.[138]

---

[138] Fr. John Hardon, SJ, "The What and Why of Mortification," *The Real Presence Association,*

Fr. Jordan Aumann, OP, notes that there are five stages to embracing suffering for the Christian. These coincide with deepening mortification:

1. Do your duty well, no matter how you feel.

2. Accept the suffering you cannot control.

3. Practice bodily mortification.

4. Prefer suffering to pleasure.

5. Offer yourself as a victim soul. (This is a special calling, not for all.)[139]

The first three stages of embracing suffering occupy the purgative way. They overlap and growth in them is cyclical. In other words, you do not have to be perfect at performing your duty before you begin working on accepting suffering and choosing light mortification. Some beginners, in their enthusiasm, try to replicate the mortification of the saints, doing lengthy fasts or hours of prayer. Often there is pride and presumption, as well as zeal, involved. It is better to proceed slowly and steadily than to try to take on too much and then fall away when you fail.[140]

When you first make a mature decision to follow God (as a convert, adolescent, or young adult), mortification should be focused on avoiding mortal sin and establishing a prayer

---

http://www.therealpresence.org/archives/Virtues/Virtues_002.htm (accessed 5/31/19).

[139] *Spiritual Theology* 2, 7.

[140] See Blessed Père Marie-Eugène, OCD, *I Want to See God : A Practical Synthesis of Carmelite Spirituality* (Westminster, MD: Christian Classics, 1989), 95.

time. The next stage is fighting against venial sin and frequenting the sacraments. A daily examination of conscience can be added here too. Another good mortification at this stage is learning to live more simply rather than storing up material goods. A good mortification for the third mansions is practicing the presence of God — that is, focusing on God's presence and goodness whatever you are doing, or at least making an effort to focus on your duty out of love for him. This practice is part of the active purification of the memory and imagination. You should refuse to linger on nonessentials, but let everything be a means to draw closer to God.

As you begin the transition to contemplation (**Question 110**), you should work further on overcoming your disordered attachments. It becomes a mortification to persevere in the dry and tedious prayer you are experiencing. You must pay close attention to what the Holy Spirit is showing you about the state of your soul and work to overcome the sin you did not recognize previously.

Another way of looking at this progression is working on what the saints call "custody of the senses." Fr. Hardon defines the custody of the senses this way:

> In Christian asceticism the practice of controlling the use of the senses, especially the eyes, in order to foster union with God and preserve oneself in virtue is founded on the premise that "nothing is in the mind that was not first in the senses." Sense experience inevitably produces thoughts in the mind; thoughts become desires; and desires lead to ac-

tions. Morally good actions, therefore, ultimately depend on a judicious guard of sensations.[141]

Custody of the senses can begin with simple practices such as not reading the tabloid headlines in the grocery checkout line. It can include limiting digital media, keeping the radio off in the car, giving up channel surfing, and being careful of what you watch and read. The eventual goal is to use your senses only in a way that draws you or others closer to God and gives him glory.

Once you are well into the passive night of the senses, the Holy Spirit will begin asking of you more radical (and perhaps what seems to be unreasonable or ridiculous) mortification. Check with your spiritual director if possible before implementing these deeper mortifications.

99. How can I keep from becoming attached to something new?

Detachment grows along with love of God. The more you love God above all else, the easier it is to put aside activities that do not correspond to his will, or to moderate those that are legitimate. But some people focus too much on the negative and are left empty. If, for example, you decide to give up reading fiction except just before bed, you might find yourself looking for another form of fun or relaxation to fill the time.

In order to keep from being attached to something new, you can look at what the saints advise for overcoming sin.

---

141 "Custody of the Senses," *Catholic Dictionary*, https://www.catholicculture.org/culture/library/dictionary/index.cfm?id=32919 (accessed 5/31/19).

They teach that when you are tempted to sin, you should practice the opposite virtue.[142] For example, if you are tempted to pride, you can take up some menial, humbling work. Now you are no longer just turning away from a bad choice, but turning toward a better choice.

To apply this to attachments, ask yourself why you should be spending less time in your pet activity. Is spending time on Facebook keeping you from getting the dishes done or spending time with your spouse? If you fill the time with what you should be doing, there is less room for forming new bad habits. If you are already fulfilling all your duties well, perhaps the Lord wants you to spend more time in prayer or take up some charitable work.

100. What should I do if I fall back?

The unfortunate truth is that almost everyone falls back at some point. Even Teresa of Ávila did so. When you recognize that you have fallen, rather than trying to stir up an emotional response, simply repent and start again. The more you fall in love with Jesus, the less often you will regress. Teresa says:

> I stress this, so that none of those who have begun to do mental prayer should stop again with the excuse that "If I am falling back into sin and still continue to pray, it will be even worse." I think it would be worse if they abandoned their mental prayer and did not correct the sin; but if they do not abandon mental prayer, let them believe that this prayer will lead them to the harbor of light. The devil waged

---

[142] See, for example, *Introduction to the Devout Life* 3, 1.

such a combat against me with that purpose…. He knows, the traitor, that whoever perseveres in mental prayer is lost to him, that all the falls he may cause them only help them, through God's goodness, to spring back even higher in God's service; so it matters to him a lot.[143]

The Devil would also have you castigate yourself over your failings. God would have you humbly recognize that you are a weak sinner and get on with the business of submitting more and more to him. Saint Thérèse of Lisieux is a master of this doctrine of benefiting from your falls. See my book *Trusting God with St. Therese* for more details.[144]

---

[143] *Life* Chap. 19, quoted by Fr. Jacques Philippe in *Time for God* (NY: Scepter, 2008), 37-38.
[144] Available at major online retailers in paperback and ebook formats.

Contemplative Prayer

101. Is meditation the same thing as contemplation?

Many people use the two terms interchangeably, but the Carmelite doctors of the Church (Teresa of Ávila and John of the Cross) distinguish between them. For them, meditation is an active prayer, in which you ponder the truths of the Faith. Contemplation is a prayer God infuses — pours in to the soul. You can and should practice meditation. You can only prepare for and accept contemplation. (See **Question 8**.)

102. What are alternate understandings of the word contemplation?

The various uses can be confusing. Here are five different ways the word *contemplation* is understood outside the Carmelite tradition:

1. Guigo the Carthusian, in his twelfth century work *Ladder of Monks* used the term *contemplatio* for the final of the four steps of Lectio divina (see **Question 34**). *Contemplatio* is a resting in God as a result of the prayer that flowed from your meditation on Scripture. In this resting, you let the

Word of God sink deeply into your heart. God can at this time lift you up beyond the reach of your faculties. In Guigo's teaching, **both the active and passive forms of resting in God** were designated *contemplatio.* This way of using the word *contemplation* to designate all non-discursive prayer was prevalent before the Carmelite doctors. Today many Catholic teachers and authors, and even whole religious orders, rely on the older, pre-John-and-Teresa understanding of *contemplation.* The Catechism sometimes uses the word *contemplation* in the more general sense as well.

2. Contemporary Jesuits use the word as a **synonym for** *meditation,* in particular, the imaginative meditation popularized by Saint Ignatius.

3. After the death of Saint John of the Cross, Venerable Thomas of Jesus was the preserver and first interpreter of the saint's writings. Thomas coined the term *acquired contemplation* **to describe the fullest development of active prayer.** Since the nineteenth century, there has been an ongoing debate among theologians and teachers of Catholic spirituality regarding the legitimacy of the term *acquired contemplation.* The term seems to return contemplation to the more general definition of non-discursive prayer that preceded John and Teresa. See **Question 108** for more on acquired contemplation.

4. A newer understanding of the terms *contemplative prayer* and *contemplation* arose in the mid-20th century. Some individuals and groups began to teach certain techniques as a means to union with God that were highly influenced by

eastern religions. Centering Prayer and the Christian Meditation of Fr. John Main and Fr. Laurence Freeman are the two most prominent examples of this phenomena in Europe and North America. These movements **sometimes make a false distinction between contemplative prayer and contemplation,** teaching that the former is a matter of changing one's awareness through thought-control techniques, while the latter is the goal, **"a state of no-thought."**[145] Such an understanding of contemplation is completely foreign to the tradition of Catholic spirituality. Teachers of Centering Prayer do not have a solidly developed theology, nor a consistent definition of terms. Sometimes they speak of Centering Prayer as acquired contemplation, other times as contemplative prayer. Fr. Basil Pennington said, "Centering Prayer is not only an opening to contemplative prayer but it is often contemplative prayer." In this case he was using the term *contemplative prayer* as a synonym for *contemplation.*[146] Centering Prayer practitioners sometimes equate their method with the prayer of quiet, which is a purely infused prayer. Although these new movements use traditional Christian terms to speak of their practices, they essentially reduce contemplation to something that can be

---

[145] Fr. Thomas Keating, *Open Mind, Open Heart.* Keating, et.al., would not themselves describe their methods as "thought-control techniques," but that is in fact what they are. See my book, *Is Centering Prayer Catholic?* for a thorough critique of the errors of Centering Prayer.

[146] James Arraj and Philip St. Romain, *Critical Questions in Christian Contemplative Practice,* www.innerexplorations.com/catchspmys/Critical_1.htm (accessed 5/31/19). I do not recommend this source for learning about contemplation as it contains many problematic assumptions.

gained by man's action, with no need for conversion of heart. See the section **Meditation: Christian Versus Non-Christian** for more on these movements.

5. Practitioners of Buddhism and Hinduism tend to use the word *contemplation* to mean **something closer to what we call *meditation*** — either pondering a subject deeply (discursively) or holding it gently within one's mind without consciously reflecting on it.

To sum up, since the deaths of John and Teresa, rejection of the use of their narrow definition of contemplation has allowed numerous errors and confusion to flourish. In the seventeenth century, the heresy of quietism arose. It led to suspicion against any talk of contemplation or the mystical life. In the nineteenth and twentieth centuries, a renewed interest in contemplation brought a renewed debate over the meaning of the term. Using the older meaning of *contemplation* since then has allowed the rise of neo-quietism in Centering Prayer and John Main's "Christian Meditation."

To preserve the authentic Catholic teaching on prayer, and to make discussion on prayer intelligible, it is best to retain the strict meaning that John and Teresa ascribed to the word *contemplation*.

103. Is speaking in tongues contemplative prayer?

Speaking in tongues and other Charismatic gifts are given for building up the Church (see 1 Cor 12 and 14). They belong to a category Saint Thomas Aquinas called *gratiae gratis datae* — graces gratuitously given. They are not given based on the holiness of the recipient, nor do they make the recipient holy.[147] Instead, they are given to make *others* holy.[148] Charismatic gifts are, therefore, extraordinary. They are outside of the normal path of sanctification and unnecessary for living a fully Christian life. Too much emphasis on these gifts can hamper spiritual growth.

Contemplation, on the other hand, is not only within the normal way to sanctity, it is itself the normal means of sanctity. Contemplation is purely God's action. It belongs to the category *gratiae gratum facientes* — gifts that sanctify the recipient. God gives contemplation only to those who have sufficiently prepared themselves. Since all are called to salvation, all are at least implicitly called to contemplation[149] (see **Question 111**).

104. Is contemplation the same thing as hearing God speak to me?

In contemplation, you often receive an obscure knowledge about yourself, and later about God or the truths of the Faith, but not in the form of concepts or images. This knowledge cannot be reduced to words. The soul does not usually recognize that the knowledge has been given, until outside of prayer. It is a knowledge of God that comes from experiencing a communion with him in prayer.[150] See the

---

[147] Aumann, *Spiritual Theology* 2, 14.
[148] Dr. Ludwig Ott, *Fundamentals of Catholic Dogma* (Rockford: Tan, 1974), 221.
[149] Aumann 2, 12.
[150] See Blessed Père Marie-Eugène, OCD, *I Am a Daughter of the Church: A Practical Synthesis of Carmelite Spiritualty* (Westminster, MD: Christian Classics: 1989), Chap. 2.

section **Listening to God in Prayer** for more on ways God may speak to you.

105. How can I attain contemplation?

If you mean how can you take possession of it, contemplation is not something you can attain in that sense. You can only prepare for it. God gives it to whom he wills, when he wills.

How can you prepare for it? Be faithful to daily mental prayer. Strive to follow God's will throughout the day to the best of your ability. Frequent the sacraments. The more faithful you are in these practices, the better prepared you are for contemplation. However, God does not owe contemplation to anyone. Even if you think yourself perfectly prepared, he may keep you waiting weeks, months, or years. In such a case, all you can do is continue to work patiently on further conversion. Humility and patient perseverance are two of the most important virtues for growing in holiness. The waiting is part of the preparation.

106. Can a person experience contemplation outside of mental prayer?

Yes. In fact, Saint Teresa indicates this in her third chapter on the fourth mansions in *Interior Castle.* She writes:

> Sometimes before one begins to think of God, these people are already inside the castle. I do not know how or in what way they heard their shepherd's whistle. It wasn't through the ears, because nothing is heard. But one noticeably senses a gentle drawing

inward, as anyone who goes through this will observe, for I don't know how to make it clearer.

Teresa probably has mental prayer time in mind in this passage, but her words can equally apply to being drawn to God while in the midst of other activities. Contemplation will most often, at least at first, occur during mental prayer, but it could occur any time God wills it. Eventually, if you reach the heights of the spiritual life, you will be in constant union with God. Then you will fulfill Saint Paul's command to "pray constantly."[151]

107. Can contemplation happen during Mass?

Contemplation can occur whenever and wherever God chooses to give it. Deep union with God should take place during the Mass, but contemplation is not necessary in order for this to happen. Blessed Marie-Eugène, OCD, says that there are three ways to intimate union with God. The first (in hierarchical order) is the Eucharist, the second is contemplation, and the third is supernatural obedience[152] (obeying authority with the motive of obeying Christ himself). Jesus reserves nothing from you in the Blessed Sacrament. He gives himself fully. If you fully gave yourself to him in preparation for the reception of the Eucharist, you could theoretically become a saint through one Communion. However, very few people would be able to prepare themselves so perfectly without having a deep prayer life, usually one that includes contemplation. More frequently,

---

[151] 1 Thes 5:17.
[152] I Am a Daughter of the Church 152-3.

your reception of the Eucharist becomes more efficacious as your prayer deepens.

In addition to the union offered in the Eucharist itself, it is not unusual for someone who regularly experiences contemplation to be drawn into that prayer when making thanksgiving after Communion.

108. What is acquired contemplation?

Many respected theologians and spiritual writers have used the term *acquired contemplation* for the final active grade of prayer (see **Question 82**), more properly known as *acquired recollection* or the *prayer of simple gaze*. The term is a misnomer. Neither Teresa of Ávila nor John of the Cross used this term. For them, it would be a contradiction. The contemplation they taught about was always infused, a pure gift of God. Nothing you do could suffice for acquiring it.

Fr. Jordan Aumann explains the history of the term *acquired contemplation:*

> In the seventeenth century some writers began to call this prayer [simplified prayer at the end of the purgative way] acquired contemplation. Saint John of the Cross and Saint Teresa of Ávila never used that expression, and ... many authors now restrict the word contemplation to the mystical grades of prayer. This is more faithful to the language of Saint John of the Cross.[153]

Meditation simplifies as you pass through the purgative way. It changes gradually from discursive meditation to af-

---

[153] *Spiritual Theology* 2, 12.

fective prayer to acquired recollection. All these prayers are active. They begin with using the senses (exterior or interior) to fill the mind with thoughts of God. See **Question 84** for more details.

Contemplation is prayer in a completely different mode. It is given by God, bypassing both the exterior and interior senses.

The term *acquired contemplation* is apt to confuse people on two levels. First, it obscures the stark difference between active and infused prayer.[154] This, in turn, can lead people toward the errors of Centering Prayer and other methods of pseudo-contemplation (see the section **Meditation: Christian Versus Non-Christian**). Second, individuals who believe contemplation can be either active or passive may have a hard time understanding what Teresa and John mean when they speak of contemplation.

109. How is acquired recollection different from infused recollection?

Saint Teresa speaks of two types of recollection: infused recollection, and a recollection which she says "is not yet supernatural."[155] This latter is what is now commonly called *acquired recollection*. Teresa speaks of infused recollection by saying:

> There is a kind of recollection, which I believe, is supernatural. There is no occasion to retire nor shut

---

[154] Admittedly, the person first receiving infused recollection may not notice this difference. But as contemplation deepens, it becomes clear that God is initiating the prayer, rather than the action of the soul.

[155] *Way of Perfection* Chap. 29.

the eyes, nor does it depend on anything exterior. Involuntarily, the eyes suddenly close and solitude is found. Without any labor of one's own, the temple of which I spoke is reared for the soul in which to pray. The sense and exterior surroundings appear to lose their hold while the Spirit gradually regains its lost sovereignty.[156]

The main difference between the two prayers, then, is that the acquired recollection is a result of some reflection, image, memory, or experience of the senses. Infused recollection is given by God when he chooses. Sometimes the one prayer may blend into the other, but at first people generally cannot distinguish between them. It is only in looking back, after they have fully entered into the prayer of quiet, that they can see that they have been experiencing contemplation for some time.

110. What does one experience when transitioning from meditation to contemplation?

John of the Cross gave three signs that one is transitioning from meditation to contemplation:

1. Meditation becomes difficult to impossible.

2. You find no consolation on the sense level in either the things of the world or the things of God.

3. You feel drawn to sit in silence during prayer.[157]

---

[156] *Interior Castle* 4, 3.
[157] *Ascent of Mt. Carmel* 2, 13.

People at this stage often feel like they are being idle in prayer and worry that they are moving backward. They begin to see the depths of their sin more clearly. This adds to their distress about their spiritual state. At the same time, their desire for God increases. They want nothing but to be near him. Since he seems absent in their prayer time, they begin looking for him everywhere, becoming increasingly aware of the way God is working in their lives outside of prayer. They are careful about committing the least offense against God.

This passive night of the senses, as John calls it, usually lasts for years. Gradually, most people begin to receive a sweeter, delicate contemplation.

See **Questions 92-95** for more on this transition period.

111. Does God call everyone to contemplation?

Yes. The Fathers of Vatican II wrote:

> Fortified by so many and such powerful means of salvation, all the faithful, whatever their condition or state, are called by the Lord, each in his own way, to that perfect holiness whereby the Father Himself is perfect.[158]

How do we grow in holiness? Through prayer and the sacraments. It follows, then, that to reach perfection in holiness, the greatest of sacraments (the Eucharist) and the deepest personal prayer (contemplation) are necessary. The Catechism says:

> Spiritual progress tends toward ever more intimate union with Christ. This union is called "mystical"

---

[158] *Lumen Gentium* no. 11.

because it participates in the mystery of Christ through the sacraments — "the holy mysteries" — and, in him, in the mystery of the Holy Trinity. God calls us all to this intimate union with him, even if the special graces or extraordinary signs of this mystical life are granted only to some for the sake of manifesting the gratuitous gift given to all.[159]

Contemplation is the full flowering of salvation in Christ. It is the means of union with God, preparing you to see him face to face. God desires the very deepest union with every human being. In creating you, he calls you to these heights. However, you must respond by continual and complete conversion. Most people, even devout Christians, hold something back from God and in so doing keep God at arm's length.

112. Is contemplation rare?

There are two ways of answering this question. If you look at the percentage of all those who call themselves Christian and who regularly experience contemplation, the answer must be, "Yes. Contemplation is rare." Saint John of the Cross says that even among those who devoutly practice prayer, less than half reach the illuminative way[160] (see **Questions 83 and 93**).

On the other hand, in sheer numbers, there are many people in the world today, even among the laity, who experience contemplation. Spiritual directors working with those who devote themselves to prayer can testify to this.

---

[159] CCC no. 2014.
[160] *Dark Night* 1, 9.

The way is long and hard and "few find it."[161] Yet, Saint Teresa encourages her readers with these words:

> Remember, the Lord invites us all; and, since He is Truth Itself, we cannot doubt Him. If His invitation were not a general one, He would not have said: "I will give you to drink." He might have said: "Come, all of you, for after all you will lose nothing by coming; and I will give drink to those whom I think fit for it." But, as He said we were all to come, without making this condition, I feel sure that none will fail to receive this living water unless they cannot keep to the path.[162]

113. Were all canonized saints contemplatives?

The controversial answer to this question is not simple, but it is a qualified *yes.*

Contemplation is the normal means to sanctity. Only through the infused graces that God gives with contemplation can a person practice heroic virtue. Such heroic virtue is necessary for canonization.[163] So, in the normal way of things, in order to become a saint, one must experience contemplation.

Of course, God can work outside the norm as he chooses. He may do so in the case of some martyrs and child saints. The common thread is that *all* saints must surrender themselves completely to the Lord. With increasing surrender of

---

[161] Mt 7:14.
[162] *Way of Perfection* Chap. 19.
[163] "The Process of Beatification and Canonization," https://www.ewtn.com/johnpaul2/cause/process.asp. Accessed 6/1/19.

yourself, God increasingly gives himself to you, which is what happens in contemplation.

You should expect that your life will follow the norm rather than be the exception. That means you should not aspire to sanctity without contemplation.

Fr. Reginald Garrigou-Lagrange, one of the greatest spiritual theologians of the twentieth century, made this point clear:

> When we say that, according to Saint John of the Cross, infused contemplation is necessary for sanctity, we mean a moral necessity, in other words, that in the majority of cases sanctity will not be attained without it. And we even add that without it the soul will not actually have the full perfection of the Christian life, which implies the eminent exercise of the theological virtues and of the gifts of the Holy Ghost which accompany them.[164]

Why do people object so strongly to this truth? First, because they misunderstand what contemplation is. If you view contemplation as an extraordinary grace, you will see it as fundamentally unjust to say that those who never receive this gift cannot be saints. But contemplation is not extraordinary. Second, many saints left little record of their prayer life. Some objectors look at the lack of record and assume that if a saint did not make his deep prayer life known, it did not exist. They should rather assume that even those about whose prayer lives they know little loved the Lord so much that they quietly spent time with him in

---

[164] *The Three Ages of the Interior Life: Prelude of Eternal Life* (Rockford: Tan, 1989), Vol. 2, 568. The author is referring to an earlier article published by Fr. Alexander Rozwadowski on the subject.

deep prayer. Third, some fear that they will never receive contemplation themselves, which means they will never attain to sanctity. But the doctors of the Church teach that those who persevere will reach union with God, even if only on their death beds (see **Question 112**).

Most Catholics have no idea of the depth of their personal weaknesses and their need for infused graces. A person can believe he is almost a saint while he is still in the purgative way (see **Question 83**), because he is living a life that is much more in accord with the Gospel than that of people around him. If he never acknowledges his need for God to directly intervene and change him at a deep level, he will likely never receive the gift God so desires to give.

114. Why does God give some the gift of contemplation, but not others?

Both Saints John and Teresa address this question, and their answers are remarkably similar. Saint Teresa writes in *The Way of Perfection*:

> Remember, the Lord invites us all; and, since He is Truth Itself, we cannot doubt Him.[165]

So the answer cannot be, "God shows favoritism to some." He does not call without giving the grace to answer the call.

Earlier in the same book, Teresa speaks of those who seem incapable of experiencing contemplation. She says someone must be Martha, and you should not worry if God calls you to active service rather than contemplation. This

---

[165] *Way of Perfection* Chap. 19.

seems to imply that God does not call everyone to contemplation. And yet, Teresa ends that section by saying:

> Be sure that if you do what lies in your power, preparing yourself for contemplation with the perfection mentioned, and that if He doesn't give it to you (and I believe that He will give it if detachment and humility are truly present), He will save this gift for you so as to grant it to you all at once in heaven... The judgments are His, there's no reason for us to become involved in them.[166]

John of the Cross writes:

> Those who do not walk the road of contemplation act very differently. This night of the aridity of the senses is not so continuous with them.... God places them in this night solely to exercise and humble them, and reform their appetite lest in their spiritual life they foster a harmful attraction toward sweetness. But he does not do so in order to lead them to the life of the spirit, which is contemplation. For God does not bring to contemplation all those who purposely exercise themselves in the way of the spirit, nor even half. Why? He best knows."[167]

---

[166] Ibid. Chap. 17.
[167] *Dark Night* 1, 9.

Elsewhere he says:

> What is lacking is not that You, O my God, desire to grant us favors again, but that we make use of them for your service alone and thus oblige You to grant them to us continually.[168]

From these passages, we can make a few conclusions:

- God invites everyone to contemplation.
- Humility, detachment, and perseverance are necessary in order to receive this gift continually.
- You should let God be God.

If you wonder why others are receiving this gift and you are not, ask yourself if you are somehow holding back from God. Do you think you deserve contemplation, as though you can earn it by your works? Such an attitude reveals a lack of humility. Are you still clinging to something other than God? He does not give himself to those who do. Work on detachment and humility, then be patient and let God bring you to a closer intimacy with him when he deems you are ready.

If you are wondering why God has granted you this gift and not others, remember Jesus' words to Saint Peter: "What is that to you?"[169] Remain humble and grateful, and pray that God bestows contemplation on all people everywhere.

---

[168] Ibid. 2, 19.
[169] Jn 21:22.

115. *Should people refer to themselves as con-templatives?*

It depends on the circumstances. Religious orders that are dedicated to prayer are known as *contemplative orders.* Members will sometimes refer to themselves as contemplatives. In this case, they are not proclaiming anything about their personal stage of prayer, but rather the goal to which their life is tending.

Individuals who are not members of a contemplative order should generally refrain from calling themselves *contemplatives.* First, many people mistakenly think themselves at a higher stage of spirituality than they are. Without a spiritual director, it is very difficult to accurately assess your spiritual state. Second, since God hides himself from those he is drawing to deeper prayer, such people feel drawn to hide themselves as well. They don't want to bring any attention to themselves. They have a profound humility. Declaring themselves to be contemplatives shines light on themselves rather than on God. They would rarely speak openly about their prayer experiences unless it was necessary to do so. Finally, calling yourself a contemplative can be presumptuous. Contemplation is a pure gift. It isn't something that you own, that is part of your identity. God could take away the gift any time he chooses.

Those who call themselves contemplatives are often practicing some method such as Centering Prayer (see **Questions 76-80**). Mistaking what contemplation is, they believe they can practice it through following certain steps. But no method of prayer or thought control can make one a contemplative without radical surrender to God.

116. What are the different levels of contemplation?

There are five levels or grades of contemplation. They are:

1. **Infused recollection:** This prayer begins at the end of the purgative way, as you are transitioning to the illuminative way (see **Question 83**). The infusion of God's life and love is so subtle that you usually cannot recognize it until you are well on your way to the next stage. Infused recollection alternates with the dry, dark prayer of the passive night of the senses (see **Question 93**). God draws your attention to himself in a simple gaze that you did not produce by any action such as meditation.

2. **The prayer of quiet:** The second contemplative prayer signals that you have now entered the illuminative way, leaving the purgative way behind. In reality, it is not a new prayer, but a longer and more intense recollection. You may still experience the passive night intermittently for a time.

3. **Simple union:** Teresa of Ávila calls this prayer *union* and places it in her fifth mansions. The soul experiences "the sleep of the faculties," in which God suspends the intellect, memory, and imagination. Union grants a certitude about God's presence.

4. **Spiritual betrothal:** Also called *conforming union*, at this stage God pledges that the soul will reach the heights of the spiritual life.

5. **Spiritual marriage:** Also called the *transforming union*. This is the last stage before seeing God face to face in heav-

en. A person who reaches the spiritual marriage will not have to go to Purgatory. He is constantly aware of God and truly lives only for God (although his faculties cannot all be constantly absorbed by God in this life, since he must engage in activities that require his attention). He can say with Saint Paul, "I no longer live, but Christ lives in me."[170] He never refuses God anything.

---

[170] Gal 2:20.

Miscellaneous Questions

117. *Do I really need a spiritual director?*

Saint Francis de Sales writes:

> When young Tobias was told to go to Rages, he said,
> "I do not know the way at all." His father replied,
> "Well go and find someone to be your guide." (Tobit
> 5:2, 4) Similarly, I say to you, dear Philothea: If you
> want to set out earnestly on the path of devotion,
> find some good person to guide and direct you. This
> is the most important advice. The devout Ávila[171]
> writes that in whatever way you search you will
> never find the will of God with such certainty than
> by following the path of this humble obedience so
> much recommended and practised by all the devout
> persons of the past.[172]

Having a director gives you the opportunity to practice
supernatural obedience, which Blessed Marie-Eugène, OCD,
says is the third way to union with God (following the Eu-

---

[171] Saint John of Ávila.
[172] *Introduction to the Devout Life* 1, 4,

charist and contemplation).[173] Supernatural obedience means obeying another person out of pure love for Christ.

Having a director also helps you to determine where you are in the spiritual life, and gives you an objective view of your spiritual state.

118. How can I find a spiritual director?

Navigating the Interior Life by Dan Burke is a book centered on the need for spiritual direction, how to find a director, and what to do while you are still looking for one. I highly recommend it. Dan also has many posts at his website SpiritualDirection.com covering this topic. In the meantime, you could try contacting a nearby religious order, a retired priest, or an association of the faithful in your diocese. You can also ask people you know who are pursuing a life of prayer if they can recommend a spiritual director.

119. Why don't priests teach about mental prayer?

Few seminaries teach Spiritual Theology anymore. Most priests simply do not have the knowledge about mental prayer themselves to teach it to others. Some priests may think the subject is too difficult for the average parishioner to understand, so they decide not to teach about mental prayer from the pulpit. This is beginning to change. Please pray that the teaching on mental prayer becomes more widespread.

---

[173] *I Am a Daughter of the Church* 152-3.

120. Do non-Catholics have different ideas of prayer and prayer methods?

This is a very broad question, the scope of which is beyond this book. Here are a few, brief points. Eastern Christians often practice methods of prayer that have a surface resemblance to non-Christian meditation techniques. Roman Rite Catholics should generally refrain from taking up eastern prayer forms such as the Jesus Prayer, unless they do so under spiritual direction. The Jesus Prayer can easily be misunderstood as a kind of mantra[174] (see **Questions 74 and 75**).

Some Protestants, particularly Evangelicals, have an interest in Catholic teaching on prayer. They read Teresa of Ávila and John of the Cross and try to put their teachings into practice. A few prominent Evangelicals have taught similarly about a deepening prayer life. A small percent of the members of the Facebook group Authentic Contemplative Prayer, for whom in particular this book was written, are Evangelicals.

Many Protestants from more liberal denominations, such as Episcopalians and Methodists, and those who identify themselves as part of the Emerging or Emergent Church, have succumbed to the errors of Centering Prayer (see **Questions 76-80**). Leaders of various mega-churches similarly have been taught this false interpretation of the Catholic tradition.

---

[174] Dionysios Farasiotis, "The Jesus Prayer and the Hindu Mantra," OrthodoxPrayer.org, http://www.orthodoxprayer.org/Articles_files/Farasiotis-JesusPrayer-HinduMantra.html (accessed 6/1/19).

For many Fundamentalist Protestants, any kind of prayer that is not explicitly taught in the Bible is suspect. Since their theology has little room for growth in holiness, it has little room for growth in prayer. They see contemplation as pagan, perhaps New Age. It doesn't help that they equate contemplation with Centering Prayer. Some of these Fundamentalists pray with Scripture. Others make use of what the Catholic Church calls *forms of prayer*: adoration and blessing, petition, intercession, thanksgiving, and praise.[175] Unfortunately, their lack of understanding that holiness is progressive keeps many in the beginning stages of mental prayer.

121. I seem to be growing lukewarm about prayer. How can I reignite the fire?

There are several things you can do to retrieve your zeal. Instead of giving in to what Saint Ignatius calls *desolation* (see **Question 50**), take up an added mortification or other spiritual practice, such as:

- Reading a spiritual book for fifteen minutes daily.
- Praying for a return of zeal.
- Asking the Blessed Mother for help.
- Meditating on the shortness of life.
- Meditating on the goodness of God.
- Using the Psalms as the basis of your mental prayer.

---

[175] CCC nos.2626-43. Of course, Protestants take these prayer forms from the Bible, not from the Catholic Church.

Remember that desolation is temporary and that through perseverance your zeal will return.[176]

122. Is Bible study helpful for deepening my prayer life?

A basic understanding of the Bible is helpful for mental prayer. A deeper Bible study can increase your knowledge of the Faith and love for God. Bible study certainly supports a growing prayer life. The knowledge learned in study can be the basis of the love that is cultivated in prayer. Do not forget, however, that in prayer itself you are meant to talk to God, not read resource materials about him. In prayer you should focus on the knowledge that will lead you to surrender more of your heart to him, rather than on the knowledge that could make you a scholar.

123. Can my temperament make mental prayer more difficult?

Yes, and it can also make it easier — no matter which temperament you have. Each of the four classical temperaments has areas in which spiritual growth is harder and also easier.[177]

For the sanguine, exterior distractions, neglecting to make time for prayer, lack of discipline in prayer, and shallowness in meditation could be a problem. On the other hand, the sanguine is likely to pass quickly from discursive

---

[176] For more help in overcoming desolation, see *The Discernment of Spirits* by Fr. Timothy Gallagher.
[177] See my book series for Catholic parents, *A Spiritual Growth Plan for Your Children*, for more on the temperaments.

meditation to affective prayer (see **Question 84**). He is also likely to have a great affection for Jesus, which could help him advance quickly.

For the phlegmatic, establishing a habit of prayer could be difficult, and also putting in the work of discursive prayer. He may give up in the face of difficulty. He can be filled with self-doubt. Like the sanguine, however, he is likely to express affection for God in prayer early on and be motivated by love of Jesus. When he reaches the transition stage to contemplation, he will more easily assume a receptive attitude than the other temperaments.

The melancholic has a strong sense of duty and yearns for the ideal or perfect. That often leads him to seek God from an early age. He also cares little about what the world thinks. On the negative side, he struggles to live in the present, may overly intellectualize prayer, have a difficult time trusting God, and succumb to pride.

The choleric is also prone to pride. He likes to be in control, so he may have a difficult time submitting to God. Agenda-driven, he can be attached to his plans. On the other hand, he is determined and almost never gives up. He works hard and makes quick progress on reaching any goals he has. His strong will may help him race through the purgative way (see **Question 83**).

People of every temperament can become saints, and many have. Increased self-knowledge can help you use your natural gifts to grow closer to God. It can also help you pinpoint your natural, temperamental weakness. Do not forget, however, that even your weaknesses may be the means of great grace. Saint Thérèse of Lisieux provides a perfect example of this truth: "for when I am weak, then I am strong" (2 Cor 12:10).

124. What does it mean to live a contemplative life?

Fr. Gabriel of Saint Mary Magdalen, OCD, defines the contemplative life as "that form of Christian life that directly seeks intimacy with God."[178] Such a life is opposed to the active life, which seeks to serve one's neighbor out of love. It's obvious that lay people living in the world, especially spouses and parents, need to live this type of active life. But the contemplative life is also possible and necessary for them.

Fr. Gabriel notes that prayer and mortification have been the traditional means of preparing oneself for supernatural contemplation. But what does that mean for the average person today?

You need to dedicate your life to prayer, setting aside thirty minutes or more (once you have established the habit) each day to spend with God. As a spouse or parent, you should primarily work on mortifying your will. What does God want you to do? How can the things you do not like about your vocation be a means of learning detachment? How can they teach you that your peace, comfort, and hope should rest in God alone?

The second way that lay people living in the world can practice mortification is by simplifying their lives. Instead of amassing possessions, you should give generously to the poor and buy and use only the things you really need. Do not forget what Jesus said about the difficulty of a rich man entering heaven![179] How much more difficult it is for them

---

[178] *Union with God* 3.
[179] Mt 19:24.

to attain holiness! Many possessions mean many distractions from God.

God calls everyone to an intimate relationship with Him, whether priests, religious, or parents of families. The path toward contemplation is simple: prayer and mortification. It is also difficult, because it entails sacrifice. Make the effort necessary to live a contemplative life and God will not disappoint you.

125. How can I find support for living a contemplative life?

With the difficulty of finding people near them who are pursuing a contemplative life, many have turned to digital communities as a substitute. I know of two that I can heartily recommend. The first is the Facebook group I started in 2016, Authentic Contemplative Prayer. At this writing, we have over 11,000 members. Posts are sharply focused on prayer and monitored for orthodoxy, truth, and clarity. I wrote this book primarily to answer the common questions we receive on Facebook. Join us at: facebook.com/groups/737852419689126/.

The second is Apostoli Viae, run by Dan Burke, President of EWTN News. Like a traditional secular order, Apostoli Viae has regular meetings, which members may attend in person or online. There is systematic teaching, a discernment process, and various levels of commitment. Learn more at apostoliviae.org/.

Acknowledgments

The blessings of God be upon all who helped me in any way with this book. First, upon my husband Dan, who patiently edits all my books and puts up with my protests to his corrections. Then upon the members of Authentic Contemplative Prayer who provided most of the questions for me to answer. Particular thanks go to my beta readers Mary Nicewarner, Becky Malmquist, Veronica Salazar, and Janice Nelson. Special thanks to Candace Gudmundson, who proofread the text for me. And to the numerous people who prayed for this project and continue to pray for me and my family — I subsist on your prayers, so thank you! Last but not least, to my sons, who pitched in to do more housework and endured my busy-ness and preoccupation while I put this book together. God reward you all with a fuller gift of himself!

About the Author

Connie Rossini lives with her husband Dan in Omaha, Nebraska, where she homeschools their four sons. Her column on prayer, "Conversation with God," is published in *The Catholic Voice* of the Diocese of Omaha. She is the author of *Trusting God with St. Therese*, the series *A Spiritual Growth Plan for Your Children,* and *Is Centering Prayer Catholic?* She also cowrote *The Contemplative Rosary* with Dan Burke. She blogs on Carmelite spirituality and raising prayerful kids at Contemplative Homeschool and is a columnist at SpiritualDirection.com. She also runs the Facebook group Authentic Contemplative Prayer.

Subscribe to Connie's blog contemplativehomeschool.com for free chapters of her other books, updates on new projects, and posts on spirituality and education.

Made in the USA
Middletown, DE
23 August 2023

37258576R00109